# Portraits
## of the Past

*Shennan Family History*

Volume 2

Compiled by

## CHRIS SHENNAN

**CP**
THE CHOIR PRESS

First published in the United Kingdom in 2023 by

The Choir Press

ISBN 978-1-78963-361-0

# Contents

# PART 1

# The Shennan Family

*By Sheriff Hay Shennan*

# Introduction

This document describes the probable derivation of the Shennan family name with a collection of early references through the centuries. It continues with a description of some of the branches of the family, along with a number of anecdotes from especially the nineteenth century.

It was prepared by Hay Shennan some time in the early 1930s, probably 1933–34. At about the same time, Hay Shennan also produced what is still (in 2022) by far the most comprehensive family tree of the Shennan family, tracing the family back to John Shennan of Auchencairn who was born in about 1740. The existing copies of that family tree were drawn up 'From data collected by Hay Shennan, and extended by his son James Hoseason Shennan, by whom this chart was prepared in Edinburgh in December 1944'.

It is clear that this description of the Shennan family and the family tree are two closely related documents.

Hay Shennan was born in 1857 and died in 1937. As is the case with Theodore Shennan's *The Old Days* (letters written in 1940 to his elder son, David), Hay Shennan's writing provides a record of the times through which he lived and about the people with whom he had contact. It is also a record of his investigations into the history of the family.

The purpose of this publication is to make Hay's document more widely available as a record of family history and of those now historic times.

Chris Shennan (David Shennan's son, Theodore Shennan's grandson)

November 2022

**Hay Shennan 1933**

Taken from his book, *A Judicial Maid-of-all-work*, published by William Hodge
and Company Ltd, Edinburgh and Glasgow.

# A JUDICIAL
# MAID-OF-ALL-WORK

BY

## HAY SHENNAN

ADVOCATE

FORMERLY SHERIFF-SUBSTITUTE AT LERWICK, DINGWALL,
DUNFERMLINE, AND HAMILTON

EDINBURGH AND GLASGOW

WILLIAM HODGE & COMPANY, LIMITED

1933

# A Sheriff Looks Back

## Scottish Life as Seen from the Bench

SO far as I am aware, our Scottish Sheriffs have not been over-ready to take the public into their confidence and write reminiscences as many other sections of the community do.

Judging by Mr Hay Shennan's *A Judicial Maid-of-All-Works* (Hodge: 7s. 6d.), the public has thereby been made the poorer; for this is one of the most entertaining books I have read for a long time.

The book-reviewer, in self-defence, develops some proficiency in the art of skipping, but, however busy or blasé he may be, I doubt whether he would wish to skip any of this volume. At anyrate, I did not wish, and did not try, to do so.

The author has been Sheriff-Substitute in Shetland, at Dingwall, Dunfermline, and Hamilton. His career, happy in many respects, was doubly so in enabling him to sample four distinctive types of Scottish life.

The Judge in his rather terrifying isolation on the Bench sees a great deal of human nature; his opportunities of studying his kind, indeed, are unique.

There is gay as well as grave in the book, and Mr Hay-Shennan has varied them in these pages with dramatic skill, and brought to bear on the whole a good deal of literary grace. Both for those who like anecdotes and those who prefer shrewd reflection on the serious aspects of life (possibly most of us prefer a due admixture of both), the book has capital attraction.

❖ ❖ ❖

THE author is an Edinburgh man, and had been in practice as a member of the Scottish Bar from 1884. He went to Lerwick as Sheriff-Substitute forty-two years ago.

Even as late as the beginning of this century the police was still a novelty in Shetland, and regarded as a rather dangerous vehicle; whereof Mr Shennan relates:—

Indeed, five years later when I was revisiting Shetland, it was still unfamiliar in the country districts. As we were cycling along a road, we saw approaching us a crofter leading a cart of peats. As soon as he saw us, he led the pony and cart off the road, and embraced the pony's head, so as to prevent it from seeing the bicycles, giving us a look of great indignation as we passed.

❖ ❖ ❖

MANY curious and amusing things happened "up there." When the author was appointed first president of the Burns Club:—

The dinner took place in a hotel, and the hotel manager had been instructed to procure a special licence for the occasion. For some reason he omitted to do so. Either he forgot, or (as I rather suspected) he considered that, as all the Magistrates and legal officials were to be present, the precaution might be safely omitted. This, however, was not the view of the Inland Revenue officials. Very properly they reported the failure to the police on the day of the dinner. In the middle of the proceedings the atmosphere of good fellowship was suddenly disturbed by the entrance of two police officers. They stood at the door for a few seconds looking at the company without saying anything, and, as I thought that possibly they wished the services of a Magistrate for some emergency, I called out, "Are you wanting me?" The reply in solemn tones was, "Not just now, sir."

The gathering collapsed in laughter, but it was only later that we knew the occasion of the visit.

❖ ❖ ❖

AMONG the many duties of the Sheriff-Substitute was that of granting warrant or the confinement in an asylum of persons medically certified as insane.

In one case where a woman was duly certified, one of the facts given as indicating insanity was that she had "smashed a new bonnet and laughed afterwards."

The author has many odd things to relate about social customs and other characteristics of life in the Highlands as seen during his stay in Ross-shire.

The Free Church ministers were a great power in the county. Of one old minister of his acquaintance the author writes:—

He was a strong supporter of the Union of the Free Church with the United Presbyterian Church in 1900. The measure was not popular in the Highlands, but he did his best to carry his congregation with him, and he was successful with the majority. He called on one recalcitrant and used all the arguments he could think of, but without avail.

At the close, as was the practice in pastoral visitation, he engaged in prayer, and in the course of it he said something like this:—" Oh Lord, Thou knowest I have been minister here for thirty years, and I have never met with such impertinence as I have to-night." Even this, however, did not avail, for the obstinate member of his flock said, "Well, Mr X., if I had any doubts before that I was right, I have none now."

On one occasion a neighbouring minister married, and it fell to this old gentleman to "preach at his "kirking," *i.e.*, the occasion when he took his bride to church for the first time after the marriage. The bridegroom, fearing a possible eulogy, made him promise that he would avoid all personal references. The promise was kept, but in his concluding prayer the old man said, "Oh Lord, Thou knowest what I had intended to say about our young friend on this occasion, but Thou knowest, Lord, that I have been forbidden."

Once in a sermon, when describing the triumph of the Gospel, he said, "Seek the Enemy of Mankind thus:— 'Roar away, Satan, roar away in silence.'" But I think one of his best efforts was when the danger of a war with the Transvaal was imminent, and the Government had sent out General Buller with troops in order to be prepared for the emergency. On a Sunday while that General was on his way to South Africa he prayed fervently that peace might be preserved, but startled some at least of his hearers by adding the qualification, "at least until General Buller arrives."

❖ ❖ ❖

MR SHENNAN was promoted to Dunfermline in 1904, and soon found himself at home among the people of Fife.

Examples of unconscious humour seem to have been common in Court there. "It's hard to say how you got implicated in a row in Lumphinnans," declared one accused person. "It was just a bit friendly quarrel," said a witness in another breach of the peace case.

One man gave an ingenious explanation of how he had come to kill a hen. "My wife told M's girl to chase the hens off the garden. They wouldn't go. I lifted a stone and it was accidental that the hen ran underneath the stone."

I liked the description given by a man in telling how he was injured "inside the eye and on the top winker." A witness in exculpation in another case declared, "Reid is not a brawler; it is more a melodious laugh." One man, not wishing to be mixed up in a brawl, explained, "He asked me in for a half, and I refused. I choose my company before my drink." Certainly many found themselves in Court because, as one witness put it, they were "awfu' spoilt wi' drink."

❖ ❖ ❖

PROMOTION again came to the author, unsolicited, in 1910. This time it was to Hamilton. One old lady wrote to the Sheriff the following testimonial:—

Dear Sir,—as I see by the papers you are going to leave Dunfermline I could not let you go without a word of thanks for your wise decision on 15th Sept. 1910. It was my big fat lazie son and I, but I have got the old age pension now and am above want now thank God for that and now to you and yours I wish you all earthly Happiness and Heavenly grace health long life for I know you have Wisdom.

Thanks to workmen's compensation cases, the Hamilton Sheriff-Substitute was the hardest worked in Scotland. Into the operation of those and other laws of outstanding social interest the writer gives us much insight.

Mr Shennan was never too busy to catch some humorous little incident, and the result is that his book abounds with such. There was the lad who described himself as a "retired schoolboy." Another tearfully pleaded, "If you let me off this time, I'll bet you a shullin' I'll no' come back."

❖ ❖ ❖

THE workings of the judicial mind are sometimes rather baffling to the layman, and the personal equation operates among Sheriffs as among lesser mortals. The following "declaration of policy" is revealing:—

The first essential in a Judge is that he shall preserve an open mind for every possible new development. Incalculable harm is done when a Judge comes into Court with his mind made up, and devotes his energies to convincing the pleaders that his view is sound, instead of giving the pleaders the chance of convincing him that their respective views are sound.

Of course, as the argument proceeds one's mind must form provisional views, but it is remarkable how these may change back and forward. Indeed the process does not stop at the public hearing. I am not alone in the experience of having sat down to write a judgment in favour of one party, only to find as the argument developed that it pointed clearly in the opposite direction.

It is most disheartening for the pleader when the Judge's attitude practically conveys the information that his arguments will be duly listened to, but will have no effect whatever. Certainly there are occasions when one's patience is severely taxed by irrelevance, and even by ignorance, but that cannot justify hasty, cocksure judgments.

❖ ❖ ❖

THE author's first principle has been to temper justice with mercy and to fit the punishment to the criminal rather than to the crime.

Vindictive sentences do incalculable harm, creating a strong anti-social bias in the victim, and evoking undesirable sympathy for him. They also sap the confidence of the community in the impartiality and far-sightedness of the Judge. What lies at the root of the vindictive is the crude idea that you do something towards righting a wrong by inflicting suffering on the wrongdoers. No social progress is to be made along these lines, and sometimes a Judge must protect the public against itself, ignoring temporary outbursts of indignation against offenders.

More than once I was criticised unfavourably for showing leniency. I never resented such criticism, for I believe it is a good thing that the public should show a living interest in the administration of the law. But I continued to err on the side of leniency (if error it be), and I did not find any bad results from this policy.

Of course, where leniency turned out to have been misplaced, a drastic sentence might follow, but this was not often found necessary. Usually offenders responded to reasonable treatment. Criminal administration may and should have a constructive aim, so that it may assist social progress. It is a poor conception that it is merely deterrent.

❖ ❖ ❖

THAT is a good note on which to end this review of a book glowing with warm humanity.

The excerpts which I have made have been chosen pretty much at random, for the quality of the author's pages is uniformly high in interest; but what I have given may afford some taste of the quality of these delightful reminiscences.

*Man o' Moray*

A review of *A Judicial Maid-of-all-work* in Theodore Shennan's copy (The Scotsman, 1933?).

# Hay Shennan's Family

*Hay Shennan was one of a number of cousins of Theodore Shennan. His immediate family was as follows:*

*John Shennan (1811–1866) was the older brother to Alexander Shennan, Theodore's father. He was married to Jessie Hay. They had a family of eight children:*

1. *John Shennan was born on 16th May 1842 in Edinburgh. He accompanied his brother-in-law, William Knox, out to Georgetown, British Guiana, where he very soon fell ill and died on 11th November 1864, aged only 22.*
2. *Mary Shennan was born on 11th July 1844. She lived into old age, unmarried, dying on 7th January 1921 in Birkenhead where she had been living with her cousin Margaret Hume for many years.*
3. *Alexander Shennan was born on 11th September 1846. He was married on 26th June 1882 to Ellen Celia Fryer and they had three children.*
   1. *His eldest son, John, was an epileptic. He was born on 23rd May 1883, and died on 25th March 1946.*
   2. *Charles Hay Shennan was born on 3rd October 1884 and died on 4th February 1940. He was married twice. His first marriage on 7th September 1921 was to Margaret Newbiggins Hay. However, she died on 16th December 1926. Charles married a second time on 21st December 1933 to Mabel Agnes Kirkpatrick. There was no issue from either marriage.*
   3. *Esher Mary Shennan born on 16th October 1889 and who died aged 55 in Gourock. She married on 1st July 1914 James Finzies Marshall, born 12th July 1888 and died, aged 79, in 1967 in Gourock. They had three sons, Leslie, Harold and Ronald.*
4. *William Shennan was born on 20th July 1848, and died in infancy on 5th August 1851.*
5. *Peter Hay Shennan was born on 23rd October 1850. He emigrated to New Zealand.*

6.  Margaret Shennan was born on 2nd October 1852 and died 11th November 1920. She married on 3rd May 1885, Robert Gibb, RSA. He was born on 28th October 1848 and died 11th February 1932. He was King's Limner for Scotland. They had no children. (Robert Gibb is mentioned in Theodore Shennan's letter to David Shennan, and was the artist of a fine drawing of Jessie Shennan, who died age 21. That drawing is in Chris's house.)

7.  James (Jim) William Shennan was born on 28th March 1856 and died 30th January 1928. He was married on 11th June 1884 to Anne Hoseason. She was born on 26th December 1855 and died on 30th January 1929. They had four children.

    1.  Elizabeth Hoseason Shennan was born on the 3rd of April 1885 and died in 1972 at the age of 86. She was unmarried.

    2.  John Eric Shennan was born on 21st July 1887 and died on 25th November 1918.

    3.  Oswald Hay Shennan was born on 15th March 1892 and died in 1979 aged 87. He was married on 29th October 1924 to Helen Brown. They had no children.

    4.  Arnold Hoseason Shennan was born on 10th April 1893. He was married on 28th March 1925 to Kathleen Margaret Walker who was born in 1904. They had two children: Douglas Hoseason Shennan who was born on 27th December 1925, and Doreen Walker Shennan who was born on 28th February 1928.

8.  The youngest and eighth child was Hay Shennan (the author of the Shennan Family document) who was born on 18th September 1859 and died on 23rd January 1937. He was married on 28th December 1891 to Isabella Hoseason, the sister of Jim Shennan's wife, Anne (see above). She died on 15th September 1923. They had three children:

    1.  John Rognvald Shennan, born on 19th September 1892. He was married on 6th June 1918 to Edith Doris Walker, sister of Kathleen, Arnold Shennan's wife (see above). They had three children: John Hay Shennan, born 21st October 1920 and died 22nd August 1979. He was married on 25th March 1944 to Jean Baird. Sheila Gow Shennan born 21st May 1923 and Margaret Doris Shennan born 24th February 1925.

2. The second child was Elizabeth Alison Shennan, born 5th January 1895 and who died 5th March 1942. She was unmarried.
3. The third child was James Hoseason Shennan born 4th November 1902 and who died age 67 in 1980. He was married on 12th April 1943 to Grace Inch Muir who was born 21st February 1904 and died in 1929 aged 74 in Edinburgh. It was James Shennan who prepared the Shennan Family Tree based on Hay Shennan's data, see earlier reference.

This description of Hay Shennan's family is drawn mainly from the family tree which he drew up. It has apparently been extended by Jean Shennan, Theodore Shennan's second daughter, who died on 1st September 2021.

Jean has also recorded the following notes about Hay Shennan's children from family discussions:

## John Rognvald Shennan

He entered Fettes in 1906 and left in 1910. He became a BSc from Edinburgh in 1913. He served in World War I from 1914 to 1919. He was a Major in the Royal Engineers. He was awarded the Military Cross and twice mentioned in dispatches. He was awarded the Order of the Crown of Romania, and served in France, the Balkans, and the Caucasus. He was an AMICE in 1917. He became director of the Welsh Granite Company in Plas Celyn.

## Elizabeth Alison Shennan

She had been a schoolteacher and was unmarried. She died of TB in Edinburgh. She was described as a chronic invalid and was looked after by her brother James.

## James Hoseason Shennan

He entered Fettes in 1916 with an open scholarship. He won an open maths scholarship to Caius College, Cambridge in 1921 and was awarded first-class honours in Maths in 1923 and then in mechanical science in 1924. He became a BA in 1924 and an AMICE in 1927.

By Sheriff Hay Shennan
brought up to about 1934

## The Shennan Family.

The name 'Shennan' as a patronymic had its origin, so
far as I can discover, in Galloway. No doubt it is of Celtic
origin. The same urge of migration which took the Scoti to
Argyll would take them to the equally near Galloway. And the
racial characteristics of the Galloway folk today are more
akin to the Highland than to the Lowland Scot. You meet with
a courtesy, a charm of manner and a softness of accent which
are in contrast with the qualities of the Lowland Scot, many as
his virtues be. And the loyalty of the Highlanders to Prince
Charlie had its counterpart centuries before in the devotion to
Robert the Bruce when he wandered among the Galloway hills, a
hunted fugitive.

Mr. Donald A. Tod, Genealogist and Searcher of Records,
says that there are two main branches of the family in Scotland.
"Both of them are no doubt branches of the ancient race of
O'Seanains or Mac-Giolla-t-Seanains of Ireland; the Irish
family are now known as Shannons and Gilsons." One branch of
the family is found in Kintyre (Argyll), and the other in
Galloway. The Irish records mention MacSeanain, Lord of
Gaileanga, who was killed in 1066, and four of his successors
down to 1145 A.D. The Kintyre form of the name was MacOsennage,
or McOshenag, as appears in documents of 1505 and 1547. The
Galloway form was Aschenan under various spellings. The prefix
A is the Gaelic Ua and the Irish O', meaning 'descendant of'.
Curiously enough, the first Scottish record of this name occurs

9

# The Shennan Family

## The Shennan Family

Brought up to about 1934

The name 'Shennan' as a patronymic had its origin, so far as I can discover, in Galloway. No doubt it is of Celtic origin. The same urge of migration which took the Scots to Argyll would take them equally near Galloway. And the racial characteristics of the Galloway folk today are more akin to the Highland than to the Lowland Scot. You meet with a courtesy, a charm of manner and a softness of accent which are in contrast with the qualities of the Lowland Scot, many as his virtues be. And the loyalty of the Highlander to Prince Charlie had its counterpart centuries before in the devotion to Robert the Bruce when he wandered among the Galloway hills, a hunted fugitive.

Mr Donald A. Tod, Genealogist and Searcher of Records, says that there are two main branches of the family in Scotland. 'Both of them are no doubt branches of the ancient race of O'Seanains or Mac-Giolla-t-Seanains of Ireland; the Irish family are now known as Shannons and Gilsons.' One branch of the family is found in Kintyre (Argyll) and the other in Galloway. The Irish records mention MacSeanain, Lord of Gaileanga, who was killed in 1066, and four of his successors down to AD 1145.

The Kintyre form of the name was MacOsennage, or McOshenag, as appears in documents of 1505 and 1547. The Galloway form was Aschenan under various spellings. The prefix A is the Gaelic Ua and the Irish O', meaning 'descendant of'.

Curiously enough, the first Scottish record of this name occurs in an Argyll record – '8th October 1309. Sir Alexander de Ergadia (Argyll), by the hands of his valet Gilbert Aschenan, 1 qr. Wheat and 4 qrs. oats.' It is suggested that he may have belonged to the Galloway family.

The next record is in 1450 of sasine to Finlay Aschenan of Carnequhin, Galloway, and many Galloway records of the name follow, though the spelling varies in a remarkable manner. In the same year, the name Gilbert Aschennane appears in the records, and in 1484 Dungallo Achinyane was witness to a Wigtown charter. In 1492, a Kirkcudbright charter was witnessed by John Schenane, presbytero 'in camera D. Joh. Schenane capellani'.

In 1517 John Aschennane de Park appears as a witness, and in 1520 he appears in a similar capacity as John Schenane de Park and as John Eschenane de Park. The lairds of Park must have prospered for they added considerably to their possessions in the 16$^{th}$ century. I cannot find an estate of that name but I conjecture that it may have lain between Woodhall Loch and Loch Ken in the parish of Balmaghie. The map shows a place called Parkhill near the north end of Woodhall Loch and the lands which they acquired lay to the south near the present village of Lauriston.

In 1529, James V at Stirling confirmed a charter of the lands of Ballemak, parish of Balmage, sold to Cuthbert Aschennane, son and heir apparent of John A. de Park. The map shows Ballymack about a mile east of Lauriston.

In 1531, James V confirmed the charter of William Makgee, granting by sale to John Aschennane de Park, in liferent and Cuthbert Aschenane his son and heir apparent, in feodo, of the 2½ marklands of Tormellane, 2½ marklands of Gropdale, 2½ marklands of Kandkwik, in the parish of Balmagee, dated at Toungland 1 Dec 1531, and witnessed by James Aschenane and others. Grobdale, Tormollan Hill and Kenick are shown on the map west of Lauriston.

In 1541, James V confirmed a charter granting by sale to Robert Aschennen, a natural son of John A de Park, the markland of Bargrenane in the parish of Balmakgee. In 1531 John Eschannane is found serving on an assize at Carlingwark, relating to lands in senesc. de Kirkcudbright (i.e., Stewartry). In 1544 Cuthbert

Eschynnane served on an assize in the county of Wigtown. He had apparently succeeded his father by that time.

In 1548 on October 29th, there is an entry showing that 'Joannes Aschennan, haeres Cuthberti Aschennane de Park (qui obiit in campo de Pinkincleugh)' was served heir to the lands of Tormellan, Grobdaill, Canknok and Ballemak in the parish of Malmaghie. It thus appears that Cuthbert Aschennane fell at the Battle of Pinkie, which was fought on 10th September 1547. About this same period there are entries relating to Robert Aschenane de Dunjop, which was a farm in the barony of Tongland about three miles NNE of the village of Ringford.

John Schennane de Dunjop appears in 1570. In 1571 we find a Robert Ashennan of Culquha which lies just north of Ringford. In 1608 Robert Aschynane of that Ilk, steward-clerk of county Kirkcudbright is mentioned, no doubt the Robert Chennan of Chennanton who was on assize on 13th May 1609. Shennanton lies on the main road about five miles west of Newton Stewart.

'Ar Halyrudhous, 12th May 1587, James VI confirmed the charter by Edward, Commendator of Dundrenane, in feu-farm to Simon Aschennand in Auchynnabyne, of the 20s lands of ancient extent of Auchynnabyne (occupied by him) in the barony of Rerik ... Andrew, eldest son of Simon A., and Barnard, brother of Simon Aschennane are mentioned in the charter.' Auchnabony lies about a mile north of Dundrennan village.

There was a James Ashennan or Shennan of Knabony or Auchenknabony who died about 1657 and his lands appear to have descended to two nieces who succeeded as heirs-portioners. A son of one of these named John Cultoun made up a title to his share and we find Auchencairn House as the residence of Cultoun of Knabony. Probably this is the branch of the Shennans with which we are connected. The name is not common now.

There was a well-known Clydesdale-horse breeder, Shennan of Balig, a farm not far from Auchencairn and a Miss Shennan lived in Auchencairn in 1924. In the early years of the nineteenth century Antony Shennan, wright in Gatehouse, died there. That was the occupation of my grandfather who settled in Edinburgh.

There is evidence that the name 'Shennan' was known in Edinburgh in 1775, for 'Shennan's Close' is given in the Edinburgh Courant of 18th February 1775 as the address of a French dancing master. But in the directory (Peter Williamson's) for 1773 the same dancing master's address is given as 'Skinner's Close' so probably the Courant version was a misprint of Shennan for Skinner. No 'Shennan's Close' can be traced. (Letter from Mr Charles Boog Watson, Huntly Lodge, 1 Napier Road, Edinburgh to J.W. Shennan, 21st January 1924.)

But at a much earlier date Shennans seem to have gone a good deal further afield. I have a cutting from the 'Scotsman' with a quotation from the 'Report of the Social Statistics of Cities', compiled by George E. Waring, Junior. Part I The New England and the Middle States. Washington Government Printing Offices:

'There fell out,' says Winthrop, 'a great business upon a very small occasion. Anno 1636. There was a stray sow in Boston which was brought to Captain Keayne; he had it cried divers times, and divers came to see it, but none made claim to it for near a year. He kept it in a yard with a sow of his own. Afterwards, one Shennan's wife, having lost such a sow, laid claim to it' – and so the story is pursued for many pages.

This stray sow in the streets of Boston (and it was a white sow) is hardly less historical than the white sow which guided Aeneas to the future site of Rome. It led to the great disputes between the magistrates and the deputies in regard to the 'negative voice', and to the final separation by solemn order of the Legislature of Massachusetts into two co-ordinate branches – magistrates and deputies, or, as we now style them, Senators and Representatives.

There is a prosperous family of Shennans in New Zealand. One was at Cambridge University about 1916.

# The Shennans of Auchencairn

I cannot trace my pedigree further back than to my great-grandfather, whose tombstone is in Rerrick Old Churchyard. The existing stone was erected at my father's expense in 1866, probably to take the place of one which had decayed. The inscription is:

> In memory of John Shennan Farmer who died at Auchencairn 1817 aged 77 years. Also Janet Donaldson his wife who died at Barlocco in 1809 aged 70 years. Also Margaret their daughter who died at Standingstane 1795 aged 25 years.

The tombstones immediately alongside show that there were other families of the name in Auchencairn, although there was lack of uniformity in spelling it. 'Shannon' appears on one stone and 'Shennon' on another, and strangely enough John Shennan's eldest son appears as William Shennon. (In the end of the 17th century Cultoun of Auchencairn House married a niece of James Ashennan of Auchnabony.) The granddaughter of John Shennan of Standingstane (Mrs John) told me that he was an only son, so it is difficult to trace his connection with the other Auchencairn Shennans.

*Rerrick Old Churchyard is near Dundrennan. Dundrennan Abbey ruins are situated 2 or 3 miles from Standingstane. The Abbey was founded by King David 1 who, about 1142, invited Cistercians from Rievaulx Abbey in Yorkshire to set up a daughter house in Galloway. The abbey had over 400 years of active life, but entered a period of active decline in the early 1500s. After the Reformation in 1560, the remaining months were allowed to live out their days there. The abbey church continued to be used as a parish church into the 1600s. But by the time the remains of the abbey were taken into state care in 1842, most of its stone had been quarried as convenient and cheap building material. Much of it remains on view today in the village of Dundrennan.*

14

*Jean Shennan found:*

> *A record for Farm Horse Tax for John Shennan of 'Standing Stane'*
> *for 1797–1798; he had two horses, both 'liable in duty' costing him*
> *£0.4.6 (22 1/2p)*

*In 2016, the present farm of Standingstone (sic) is by the A711 road*
*halfway between Auchencairn and Dundrennan.*

Standingstane is a small farm about three miles south-west of
Auchencairn. I first visited it on Wednesday 22nd April 1885 and
found the buildings very much as they must have been in John
Shennan's time. The farmer told me that the threshing-mill was at
least 105 years old. In 1893 my brother Jim wrote that he found it
amalgamated with another farm, and the buildings broken down,
but in 1924 we visited it and found it in good order. It is a small
farm and stands high with a fine view from it.

I can trace only three children of this John Shennan:

1.  Margaret born probably in 1769. She died in 1795 aged 25.
2.  William born probably in 1771. He died in 1808. He married
    Janet Graham and they had two daughters: (1) Janet, who
    married Thomas John. She was born in 1805 and died 1st May
    1894. (2) Margaret, born 1807 and died 1850 unmarried.
3.  John, born in 1773 (my grandfather).

John Shennan of Standingstane had a small property (probably a
little house) at Rhonehouse, a place otherwise known as Keltonhill,
about three miles south-west of Castle Douglas. He may have had
some relationship to the John Aschennane who in November 1640
served to the lands of Mollance and Barncrosh in the parish of
Tongland, for these places are two or three miles west of
Rhonehouse. Dunjop and Culquha are just west of Mollance.

William Shennan, as the elder son, took up farming, and John, the
second, became a wright. I think it may be fairly conjectured that
William continued to assist his father at Standingstane and
perhaps succeeded him there, for his mother, Janet Donaldson,

died at Barlocca, a farm near the shore south of Auchencairn. William married Janet Graham about 1804. He died in 1808. His mother died in 1809 at Barlocca and his father died in 1817 at Auchencairn.

John appears to have settled in Edinburgh very early in the 19th century. In 1842 his brother-in-law, Patrick Lamb, spoke of having known him for forty years.

William Shennan's widow, Janet Graham of Collin, as she describes herself on the tombstone she erected to her husband in Rerwick Old Churchyard, was clearly a strong character. She lived at Collin Mill on the outskirts of Auchencairn, dying there on 5th April 1876, aged 95. Left a widow with two girls of 3 and 1 years of age, she was determined to support herself and her children without charity. She refused an offer of marriage on the ground that 'she would not feed William's children out of another man's girnel'. She never forgot William Shennan, though she survived him for 68 years.

*They are recorded in the cemetery at Auchencairn:*

*Erected by Janet Graham at Collin in memory of William Shennon (sic) her husband who died 28th August 1808, age 37 years. Also of Margaret Shennon their daughter who died 28th December 1850 aged 43 years. Also the above Janet Graham who died at Collin Mill 25th April 1876 at 95 years.*

Her granddaughter, Jenny John, afterwards Mrs Reid, told me that shortly before the old lady died she said, 'I'll soon see my dear William Shennan.' In 1885 I met a Mr Boyes in Auchencairn who remembered her when he was a boy. After school hours many of the children went to her house and she gave them a bible lesson. A fortnight before her death she gave him a book and some very wise counsel. He recalled that she used to smoke an iron pipe, this agreed with one of my early recollections.

Before every New Year my father sent a black bun to his Aunt Shennan at Auchencairn. It was packed in a square wooden box and the corners left by the round shape of the bun were filled with tobacco. The box was returned with a pair of geese, one of which was our New Year's Day dinner, while the other went to Aunt Margaret Shennan, who lived in the upper flat of Bellevue Cottage.

My Grandfather was very kind to his sister-in-law, William's widow. When he went to William's funeral, he had got some of William's clothes, and in return he gave each of William's daughters a dress every year. He had Janet (who became Mrs John) staying with him for fifteen months in the 'house in the garden' at the west end of Barony Street, Edinburgh, so that she might learn dressmaking. She spoke of John Shennan junior, my father, who was six years younger, as a 'stout' boy (meaning sturdy and strong) and always so kind.

I got this information from Mrs John when I visited her in 1885. Bella and I saw her in April 1894, but she was very frail and, I think, confined to bed. She died on 1st May 1894. Her husband was Thomas john, an exciseman of Irish extraction, who was much older than she, having been born about 1779. He died in 1860.

They had eight children. The eldest was Thomas John, a handsome man, who was a well-known teacher of English in the fashionable seminaries for young ladies in Edinburgh. His two daughters still live in Edinburgh. Another son was William John, joiner in Auchencairn, whom I met in 1885. One of his daughters was Mrs Reid, who was postmistress in Auchencairn, and we had her house, Rosebank, for August 1924. Another daughter is Mrs Mitchell, wife of the baker there. Mrs Reid amused me by expressing a not very high opinion of her grandfather Thomas John.

Mrs John was a handsome woman, strongly resembling her father in appearance, and her sons Thomas and William inherited the Shennan features. When I saw William John at Collin Mill in 1885, one of those present remarked on the strong resemblance between him and me. Many years later, when we were in Hamilton, on making my first purchase from Edwards, the Jeweller in Buchanan Street, Glasgow, I was proceeding to spell my name to the assistant who served me. He smiled and said, 'Oh, I know that name very well; my father's name was John Shennan Graham John.' I claimed kinship at once and he said, 'When you came into the shop, I said to myself that you were very like my father.' His father was Mrs John's second son who had settled in Glasgow.

As William Shennan predeceased his father, the Rhonehouse property fell to John Shennan (my grandfather) as heir. He, however, took no steps to make up a title and left William's widow to draw the rents. My father let things go on as before and she in fact outlived him ten years. We used to joke about our ancestral property in Galloway. Mrs John continued to draw the rents as her mother had done. Mrs Reid told us that the property was sold by Thomas John after his mother's death in 1894, although I am puzzled to know how he made up a title to it. The proceeds were divided among Mrs John's family, producing about £1 to each. So Mrs Reid told me.

# John Shennan 1773–1842

William Shennan was evidently intended to succeed his father as a farmer, and John trained as a wright. As we find Antony Shennan a wright in Gatehouse in 1812, it seems not unlikely that John learned his craft under a relative. I do not know how he came to settle in Edinburgh, but the name 'Shennan' was known in Edinburgh in 1775, so it may have been on the suggestion of a relative that he did so. This was early in the 19th century.

He married in 1808 Margaret Lamb, daughter of William Lamb, Builder and Joiner, Tyningham, East Lothian. He was 35 and she was 27. Her brother Patrick Lamb (her senior by 10 years) was a builder in Leith, who in 1842 wrote of his forty years' friendship with John Shennan and it was no doubt at his house that he met his future wife. Patrick Lamb lived in Coatfield Lane, Leith. John Shennan and his wife lived first in Young Street, where their two eldest children were born and then in Barony Street in 'Hogg's House', situated at the west end of the street near Broughton Market and beside the 'carriers' quarter'. It was known as 'the house in the garden'. Later they lived on the north side of Gayfield Square.

At one time he was in business as a 'Wright' with a Mr Walker, who afterwards settled in Birkenhead. The firm's name was 'Shennan & Walker' and the name remained for a time after the dissolution of the partnership, which must have been in the early 1830s. They seem to have had a good business, not confined to Edinburgh. They were engaged on Murthly Castle, Perthshire 1830–1832 and on 'Clan Gregor Castle' near Doune 1832–1833. I cannot identify this castle, but it may have been Lanrick Castle.

Then John Shennan started on his own account under the designation 'John Shennan Wright'. I remember the name above the workshop at Bellevue Cottage. He built houses in Moray Place,

Doune Terrace and Saxe-Coburg Place and also Greenside Parish Church. His eldest son, John (my father) learned the trade under the partnership, being employed at Murthly and at Clan Gregor Castle, but in 1833 went to London to gain experience.

William the second son, after a few months at sea went into his father's business, but died on 28th June 1835, and then John returned from London to assist his father. One of his jobs was to go to Ardmaddy castle, Argyll, in March 1838 to estimate for work to be done for Lord Breadalbane, but this seems to have come to nothing. A similar visit to Sunlaws near Kelso proved more successful, for they did the work there.

John Shennan Senior died on 25th November 1842 between 4 and 5 on his way home from his shop and yard (which were possibly at the west end of Barony Street), death being sudden from a heart attack. The gas bracket on the south side of Broughton Place church in the road leading from Broughton Place to Gayfield Square was pointed out to us as the place where he was found dead. 'Thus died', wrote his son John to his cousin John Lamb (a son of Patrick Lamb), 'my excellent father, a man who I believe left this world without an enemy and he had many attached and kind friends.'

He seems to have been a man of very fine character. His niece, Mrs John, in speaking of him to me said, 'To speak in a plain way, he was a good man.' The two letters of his which have been preserved show him to have been a sincerely religious man, but there was not a trace of cant about him or of the kill-joy spirit. His strong sense of humour made his home a happy one. It was from him, rather than from their mother, that his children inherited their cheery humour.

That he was not a 'heavy father' is plain from the story told me by his youngest son, Alexander. When Alexander was a small child, his father had corrected him for something or other, and the child resented it, perhaps thinking he had been unjustly treated. When it came to bedtime, the small boy said goodnight to each of the members of the family present except his father, whom he ignored. Then just as he was going out of the room either his conscience pricked him or his sense of filial duty inspired him, so he turned and said, 'Goodnight, Father, I fancy.'

There were eight children in the family, of whom William alone predeceased his father. Margaret, the eldest, was petite, but the others were of handsome build. John, the eldest son (my father), was a buirdly man standing 6 feet. It was a jolly high-spirited household, given to hospitality and there were frequent visits from cousins of Auchencairn and East Linton. Mrs John told me of an occasion when John Shennan was paying a return visit to Auchencairn with one of his daughters. His sister-in-law, Mrs William Shennan, said to him, 'I daresay, brither, ye'll be prood o' your bairns.' 'Na, na,' he replied, 'I hae muckle tae be thankful for, but naething to be prood o'.'

The two youngest daughters, Marianne and Isabella, had a great admiration for their eldest brother, John, but they were not deterred by their admiration from playing tricks on him. They used to bake small meat pies, and John always said that they were not sufficiently seasoned. So on one occasion they bought a pennyworth of pepper, and put it into one pie for him. As soon as he tasted it, he guessed the trick, and, reaching out for the cruet, said, 'This pie is excellent, if it only had a little more pepper.'

Margaret, the eldest, had a rather quick temper, which is sometimes a protection for small-statured persons. Once John said or did something which made her lose her temper, and she said, 'John, I could kick you.' John, a man of 6 feet, politely presented her with a chair to stand on, in order to achieve her desire and presented his back to her. Needless to say, wrath at once gave place to laughter, thanks to the family sense of humour. At times, they showed a pretty wit. Once a son of Mr Walker (who had been John Shennan's partner) was a guest in the latter's house, and was foolishly boasting of his forebears and telling how they used to drive their carriage and pair. Margaret's comment was, 'This I know, my grandfather drove his agricultural tandem.' It was a quaint description of the tenant of Standingstane ploughing.

John Shennan and his family attended St James's Place Relief Church, which lay west of the Roman Catholic Chapel in Broughton Street and the Theatre-Royal. He was an elder. Some time in the 1880s an old elder of that church, Mr Learmonth, told me that when he, as a young man, was appointed an elder, his first spell of duty at the collection plate in the vestibule was with John Shennan. When Mr Learmonth asked his senior what his duties were, the only advice he was given was, 'When you are asked for change, never give them bawbees.' So he carried some shrewdness into his religious duties and would not countenance anything less than a penny being put in the plate.

When John Shennan died, his affairs were found in perfect order. He left a memorandum dated 10th December 1841, explanatory of his will with various particulars of his estate. He emphasised his wish that his widow shall have every comfort. He did in fact leave enough to keep his widow and family in comfort. Only the eldest son, John, was married, so the family left at home consisted of five daughters and one son.

Here is a letter which he wrote to his eldest son, John, on his leaving home for Murthly at the age of nineteen:

Edinburgh
23rd March 1830

John,
You are now leaving your earthly Father's house, but remember your heavenly Father is everywhere present, for his eye seeth all things – he beholdeth the evil and the good. You must remember you have voluntarily devoted yourself to the Lord, by renewing your Baptism engagements at his table. Let not the world laugh you out of your religion. You have

made a noble profession and that act is recorded in Heaven; make it therefore your study never to dishonour your divine Master. I look upon the sanctifying of the Sabbath as a Christian duty which cannot be dispensed with. Be therefore a constant attendant on divine ordinances. Remember that the Wise Man saith 'Remember your Creator and Redeemer in the days of your youth.' Timothy knew the Scriptures from his youth. Samuel was early distinguished for piety – therefore take care what associates you take up with. Your education entitles you to something more than may be expected from a person wholly illiterate. Not that I would wish you to despise any person – far from it but I wish you would take care who you associate with or make your bosom friends. You know religion does not exist in mere externals. The Apostle says 'Pray always'. Not that we can always be upon our knees – but to have always a praying frame of mind. Do not therefore neglect morning and evening prayer. Do not excuse yourself by saying you want a place. A praying heart will always find a praying place. Meditation and prayer are the elements in which a Christian delights to move. Read the Scriptures not merely as a task but as the word of God to fallen man – that word which maketh wise unto salvation. Search the Scriptures, saith our divine Master, for they testify of me.

Do not let the sneer of a vain world deter you from duty. Let me tell you that by observing the above it will tend to your furtherance in life – and your respectability among men – and above all, to your comfort in death and happiness in another world. I do not wish you to be a recluse. Associate with the good and the wise. And remember a person is known by the company he keeps. You will find some serious people almost everywhere. I have found them in the heart of the Highlands – a much more unlikely place than you are going to.

There is no saying, we may never meet in this life again – but remember life is short, Eternity is long; we ought to prepare for it by every means in our power. And blessed be God, we have the means, for it is said Believe in the Lord Jesus Christ and thou shall be saved. Be watchful not only over your actions but over your words. Let no lies proceed out of your mouth. A tree is known by its fruit. Let not your lips speak guile. Beware of drunkenness – it is too much a practice to indulge themselves on a pay night. Avoid this practice. I do not say, never indulge in a social glass, but beware of drunkenness, it ill becomes a Christian.

As I hope to have future opportunities of corresponding with you, I shall now conclude, by commending you to the care of the Almighty – and may the God of peace go with you and direct your path in life. May the grace of our Lord and Saviour Jesus Christ and the divine influences of the Holy Ghost be shed abroad in your heart. May you be a vessel of honour, prepared for the service of the upper sanctuary. May your life be spent in his service, and to the honour of his name who is Lord of heaven and earth. And may you and I and all our family and all with whom we are connected in life meet at the right hand of the Great Judge on the great day of accounts and hear the Judge pronounce that happy sentence, Come ye blessed of My Father inherit the kingdom prepared for you from before the foundation of the world. What are all the pleasures of this life, in comparison of being found in Christ and having our souls sanctified by his spirit!

And now, as it appears that it is the will of God, that we should separate for a little in bodily presence, let us frequently meet at the Throne of Mercy and pray for each other's present happiness and future glory. And this is our confidence that of we pray he heareth us. May the Almighty bless you is the sincere prayer of

Your affectionate Father

John Shennan

N.B. The above are a few unconnected hints suggested to me in a leisure hour this day at the Park and I hope will not be in vain.

Probably the 'Park' was what was known as 'The Cuddies' Park', which was situated north-east of Gayfield Square. Hope Crescent was built on part of it. In my boyhood I remember the small remaining portion at the corner of Annandale Street and East London Street. I think I have seen donkeys grazing on it, and it certainly was used by travelling shows.

# The Lamb Connection

John Shennan's wife, Margaret Lamb, was the daughter of William Lamb, Wright, Tyningham, East Lothian, and his wife Margaret Thomson. William Lamb was born in 1734 and died in 1809 being buried in Whitekirk Churchyard. His wife was born in 1737 and died in 1818. They had a family of ten, of whom two died in infancy. The eldest was May, who strongly objected to being called Mysie, and expressed the wish that any child named after her should be called Marianne and this was done in not a few cases. Alexander Lamb was born in 1764, was married, and died in East Linton in 1824.

Daughters born in 1766 and 1768 died in infancy. Janet, born in 1770, married – Laurie – and settled in Athelstaneford; they had five sons and one daughter. Patrick, born in 1772, became a builder in Leith and lived in Coatfield lane there. It seems to have been through him that John Shennan met his future wife. Patrick had four sons and three daughters. William, born in 1774, was a Wright in East Linton, latterly in partnership with his younger brother James. William had a family of eleven. James born in 1778 had four daughters. Margaret was born in 1781 and she married John Shennan in 1808. The youngest was Isabella who married – Smail – and lived at Athelstaneford. She had two sons and three daughters.

The various families kept in close touch with each other and there was much coming and going between Edinburgh and East Lothian. My father, John Shennan Junior, spent many holidays as a boy among his relatives in East Lothian, his nearest contemporaries being his cousins James and Thomas Laurie and Alexander Smail. But there were other cousins in East Linton near his age and he certainly spent some of his time there in his Uncle William's hospitable house.

The boys were full of high spirits. One of their feats was to walk on the top of the high holly hedge which bounded the Tyningham House policies. In my boyhood this was a hedge ten or twelve feet high and six or more wide in firm compact condition. Now it is decayed and a mere skeleton.

In Edinburgh (according to his elder sister Margaret) John Shennan made himself champion of the smaller boys and fought their battles for them. They called him 'Cock Shennan', and used to ask at the door. 'Is Cock in?' He was at the head of most of the boyish mischief in the neighbourhood, but Aunt Margaret always added, 'There was no wickedness in his mischief, it was always straight.' Thus, when he went to East Lothian, he was likely to get into scrapes.

On one visit he stayed with an uncle who was inclined to be strict. Some practical joker told the boys that, if they rooted up all the carrots in the garden, they would 'kill the Devil'. The boys believed him and carried out the good work thoroughly. The uncle very naturally reprimanded them and the boys were so indignant at his failure to appreciate the praiseworthiness of their attempt that they made a moonlight flitting to a more indulgent uncle. One of these East Lothian uncles (Uncle Laurie, I think) owned a variety of wigs, and he used to wear a red one on Sundays.

William Lamb of Tyningham, (my great-grandfather) was buried at Whitekirk, as I have said. I was unable to find any stone marking the place. His sons transferred the business to East Linton (about two miles from Tyningham) and evidently his son William took up his father's hospitable functions.

His eldest daughter was Rebecca (1810–1891), who became Mrs Knox. Her daughter, Rebecca Lamb Knox (1844–1930), lived in East Linton and gave me much information on family matters. The great day for family reunion was Handsel Monday, when William lamb kept open house at East Linton. Miss Rebecca Knox wrote:

27

'In my girlhood I can remember my mother talking about the great Handsel Monday visits to her father's house, when the relations came from Leith by stage-coach and other relations were present, and I remember her speaking of Aunt and Uncle Shennan, Aunt Mary and Aunty Bell.'

She told me of one incident which shows the kindly, cheery lot they were. William Lamb's first wife, Helen Aitken, died in August 1829. (Miss Rebecca gave me the letter written by my grandfather John Shennan to William Lamb at the time.) It fell to Rebecca as the eldest daughter, to prepare the Scotch broth for the Hansel Monday dinner of 1830. She was very anxious to have it right. Just when it was nearly ready, she was called away by someone, and when she came back, she found it a little burnt. She was in great distress, and consulted 'Aunt Libby' (perhaps Aunt Tibbie, wife of her Uncle James) who said, 'Oh, it's nothing; they'll never notice it.' All the guests expressed great praise of the broth and came back for second helpings. Later Rebecca found out that 'Aunt Libby' had dared the guests to take any notice of the broth being burnt and had charged them all to take second helpings.

The diary which my father kept from 1830 to 1838 tells of some of these visits. After his walk from Murthly on Hogmanay 1830 he stayed some time at home, and then set off to the East Country to hold the Handsel Monday. 'It was then,' he says, 'I first saw my second Aunt William. She is a very pleasant woman and took among us very much.' (This was Agnes Stewart, widow of John Storie V.S.) 'I spent a week very happily among my friends.'

The diary tells of another episode in 1833 in the company of his cousin James Laurie, who was a year older: 'Went to the East country in the beginning of May with James Laurie. We spent a few days very comfortably with them. We visited Athelstaneford, Linton, Bogue End and Dunbar. We took rather little time but on the whole we did very well. It would not do for we two to leave the East country without committing some fault, so to keep up the old <u>look</u> we took Uncle Willie's two horses to Athelstaneford as they would not rise to let us in (it was near 12 0'clock I think). We went and took the horses and after getting something in the shape of saddles etc. we kept racing with each other until we got to Athel. We sent them back next morning just in time to save the crier a job, as Uncle Willie was wondering what had come o'er his cattle.'

Again in September 1835 he tells of a visit to Athelstaneford and East Linton where they stayed with 'Uncle Wm's family' (Uncle William died in 1834). The last morning there 'we then went to have a look at the garden where we had a bickering with the young Lambs with their apples. There were several small damages done such as knocking noses about, hats put into all shapes and other small matters too many and various to be enumerated.' He spent Handsel Monday there both in 1837 and 1838.

In years within my recollection we seem to have lost touch with East Linton, though Miss Rebecca Knox remembered being in Bellevue Cottage. The only relatives living in East Lothian of whom I remember were my father's cousin Aleck Smail, and George and Isabella Sinclair, his sister's children, who lived with him in Haddington, where he was in business as a tobacconist and tallow-candle maker. Four of 'Uncle Willie's family' emigrated to New Zealand and prospered there.

James Laurie was a shoemaker in Edinburgh. He lived in Osborne Cottage, West Ferry Road. Its front elevation was exactly the same as Bellevue Cottage, and it was situated just east of the present Dunkeld Lodge. Later it was acquired and demolished by Mr Currie, and the site was incorporated in the garden of 'The Cottage' as his house was inappropriately named.

It may have been the proximity of James Laurie which induced my father to buy the field west of Osborne Cottage with the intention of building a house for himself there. We used to call this 'the field at Windlestrawlee' and I remember a crop of potatoes being taken off it. It was feued after his death, and the site is occupied by

Dunkeld lodge, and Nos 2, 4, 6 and 8 Wardie Road. James Laurie's son settled in London and married there.

Of the family of Patrick Lamb of Coatfield lane, Leith, three sons settled in New Zealand. Another, John, was an East India merchant in Calcutta. After his death in 1867, his widow and four surviving children lived in Blenheim Place, Edinburgh and the children were among our companions. The only survivor at present (1933) is William, born 1855, a doctor in Birmingham, married with three grown-up sons. The youngest of John's family was baptised John Sinai Lamb with water brought by his father from the Jordan. He died in infancy, and we used to be told that some infection from the Jordan water was the cause of his death.

James Lamb of East Linton left a widow and four daughters who settled in Edinburgh and carried on a select millinery business first in George Street and then in Coates Crescent.

# The Family of John Shennan and Margaret Lamb

After the death of John Shennan in 1842, his widow and family stayed on in the house in Gayfield Square for some years. I think the house was on the north side of the square and I have an impression that the number was 24. In 1847 they removed to Haddington Place and in 1850 they came to the upper flat of Bellevue Cottage.

1. Margaret, the eldest, was never married. She lived on in Bellevue Cottage till we had to leave it in 1872, as the site was required for the new Catholic Apostolic Church. After 1864 Aunt Margaret had the Knox family under her charge. In 1872 she and the Knoxes lived in Annandale Street for some years. Ultimately she went to live with her sister Isabella in Birkenhead, where she died in 1888. She was born in 1809.

2. John was born in 1811. He was married in 1841 and took up house in 15 Hart Street. In 1850 he removed to Bellevue Cottage, where he occupied the ground flat, while his mother and her family occupied the upper flat. I give his family later (this is now missing).

3. Jessie was born in 1813. In June 1864 she married Samuel Edgar, a widower, who practised as a doctor in Birkenhead. He predeceased her. She died on 6th August 1890.

4. Christina Graham was born on 23rd October 1815. She married on 14th September 1847 William Knox, merchant, Georgetown, Demerara (born 14th March 1812, died 26th January 1866). He belonged to Edinburgh, where he was a glazier and he was a great friend of John Shennan. Christina Graham Knox died in Edinburgh on 9th May 1864. William Knox married a second time in Demerara to a Miss Paterson, who came from

Dalbeattie. William Knox and Christina Graham Shennan left three children:

(1) Margaret was born on 30th November 1851. She married her cousin, James Hume, on 28th December 1875. They lived first in Liverpool and then in Birkenhead and had four children:

    (a) James Edgar, born 8th March 1877. He married Wilhelmina McKean.

    (b) Christina May, born 25th May 1879, died 27th April 1886.

    (c) Isabella Margaret, born 10th April 1881

    (d) William Walter Kenneth, born 24th August 1888, died on service in France on 31st July 1917.

(2) Jeanie, born 7th May 1855. She lives with her sister at Waterloo, near Liverpool.

(3) William Arthur, born 9th March 1857. He married Janet Hay Easton on 7th August 1884 and they had one son, Arthur Easton William. William Arthur Knox died on 23rd March 1910.

5. William was born in 1817. In November 1832 he was indentured at Greenock to the Brig Mary Ann of Leith, owner Mr Cockburn. His father and his mother and his brother John accompanied him to Greenock to see him off. I think one voyage was enough to put an end to his nautical ambitions, for soon he returned home and began work as a joiner in his father's shop. He died on 28th June 1835 at Edinburgh, at a time when his brother John was working in London. In his diary the latter in referring to William's death writes of him as 'William who so often occupied my thoughts, who I had hoped would have followed me to London at some after period and for whose benefit I had been making acquaintances in the Trade, for whose benefit I had joined the Trade Society.'

6. Marianne was born in 1820. I think she was rather delicate. She went to Demerara on a visit to her sister Christina. She died there on 19th November 1851.

7. Isabella was born on 15th March 1822. She married on 25th September 1844 James Hume, Plumber, Birkenhead. He had gone to Birkenhead from Edinburgh. He was born on 18th April 1807 and died on 6th February 1854. Isabella died at Birkenhead on 9th December 1900. They had five children:

(1) James born on 21st July 1847 and died on 21st October 1904. He married his cousin Margaret Knox and their family is detailed above.

(2) John Shennan, born 27th February 1849, died 6th May 1849.

(3) William born 18th August 1850, died November 1906. He married Nellie Sclanders who died on 30th December 1913. They had no family.

(4) Alexander Shennan, born on 7th October 1852. He married on 14th August 1890 Annie Wilhelmina Robinson. They had four children:

    (a) Alison Shennan, born on 4th August 1891, died 28th August 1891.

    (b) Norah Leslie, born on 5th August 1892.

    (c) William Martin, born on 28th May 1894. He married in 1930 Constance Madge Lowe. They have one child, John Alexander, born 28th November 1931.

    (d) Kathleen Margaret, born 24th December 1898.

(5) Margaret Isabella, born 7th September 1854, died on 26th January 1930.

8. Alexander, born on 1st August 1824. He was a minister of the United Presbyterian Church, first at Houghton-le-Spring and then at Bathgate. He married on 24th April 1855 Jane Steele Lawson. She was born on 23rd March 1825 and died on 21st March 1914. He died on 13th May 1891. They had nine children:

(1) John, born on 7th March 1856. He married on 31st October 1889 Alice James and they had two children who died young.

(2) William Finlay, born on 17th September 1857, died 5th April 1873.

(3) Jeannie Steele Lawson, born on 4th June 1858, died on 19th March 1931.

(4) Margaret, born on 2nd July 1861, died on 31st January 1873.

(5) Jessie Christina Alexandra born 17th February 1863, died on 20th May 1884.

(6) Alexander *(Lex)*, born 20th January 1865. Dentist in Edinburgh.

(7) Lawson Storrow, born 10th August 1866. Dentist in Edinburgh.

(8) Isabella Elizabeth born on 17th January 1868 died on 6th May 1905.

(9) Theodore, born on 9th March 1869. Professor of Pathology in Aberdeen. He married on 30th July 1903 Minnie Green. She died on 29th April 1932. They had three children:

(a) Eileen Ivy Theodora, born on 27th November 1904, died on 12th May 1907.

(b) David John George, born on 8th March 1909. Civil Engineer.

(c) Edward Theodore, born on 27th February 1916.

He married again in July 1934, Ann Lindsay Thomson.

My grandmother Margaret Lamb or Shennan died at Bellevue Cottage, Edinburgh on 13th December 1857. She was blind for some years before her death, having been troubled for long with night blindness (retinitis pigmentosa). This defect seems to be transmitted mainly through females. There are good grounds for believing she inherited it from her mother. She transmitted it to at least three of her daughters (Margaret, Christina and Isabella) but it did not appear in her sons, and has not appeared in Christina's descendants and in Isabella's.

# Letter from Hay Shennan to Theodore Shennan

'About Maggie Gibb's blindness. The original is with Dr Usher with whom I *(Theodore)* published a paper on night blindness in 1930.'

41, Stirling Road
Trinity
Edinburgh

20<sup>th</sup> April 1929

Dear Theo

As far as I know, Maggie never consulted an oculist after her marriage, and that may account for Robert Gibb not answering you. Probably I know more of the matter than he does.

What affected her was an actual injury to the structure of the eye. It began when she was in Germany at the age of 18 and my recollection is that it was blamed on improper treatment there. In Edinburgh she was treated by Dr Walker, who shares with Dr Argyll Robertson the chief eye work then. I never heard her condition associated with night blindness and I cannot recall that her sight was worse at night than by day. The injury to the eye was quite apparent. My impression is that the condition was stabilised by the time of her marriage and long before that and I do not recall any progressive worsening. Of course we all knew of the family weakness and that makes me think that Dr Walker would be told of it. Certainly her condition never was ascribed to night blindness in my recollection.

This may help you. When I next see Robert, I shall try to remember to ask him if he can say any more, but I doubt it.

Etc. with regard to my own troubles, to Tom Hoseason and to Arnold settling in Johannesburg (sic).

Your Affectionate cousin

(Signed) Hay Shennan

Ends

# Acknowledgements

David Shennan passed a copy of the original Hay Shennan document to Chris some time in the late 1980s as part of his 'Shennan Archive'. Almost all the rest of that archive has been deposited at the Norfolk Record Office in Norwich (material that related to David's mother, Minnie Green, and her family) or at the archive of the University of Aberdeen (material that related to David's father, Theodore).

Although the original document was typed, it existed only in hard copy form. It was typed up by Jean Shennan, Theodore's daughter, who was born in 1936. After Jean's death on 1st September 2021, Chris took Jean's file with the aim of publishing it for wider family interest.

Essentially all the script is as written by Hay Shennan. Some limited editing has taken place to improve the layout and punctuation, and to make corrections.

# Introduction to Parts 2, 3 and 4

Before she died on 1st September 2021, Jean Shennan, Theodore Shennan's second daughter, was working on the history of a number of branches of the Shennan family. Although these had not been completed, there is clearly value in having them more widely circulated without waiting for possible future research.

Most of the writing is as left by Jean, but it has been extensively edited by Chris so that it follows a reasonably complete and logical order. It was clearly a work in progress and had remained so for at least 10 years.

Chris Shennan (Jean Shennan's nephew and Theodore Shennan's grandson)

November 2022

# PART 2

# John Shennan
# 1855–1939/40

*By Jean Shennan*

# Introduction

This history is about John Shennan who was the eldest of Alexander Shennan's family. He was the eldest brother to Theodore Shennan, Jean's father and Chris's grandfather. Theodore died in 1948, but it was clear from his writing (*The Old Days*, Letters from Theodore to his elder son, David Shennan, 1940) that John was considered something of the black sheep of the family.

Considering the times through which he lived, John Shennan travelled an astonishing amount, from Scotland through North America (especially Arizona and Montana) to Peru, Bolivia, and Argentina (of the countries of which we know). His character and story clearly appealed to Jean, and it was of some delight to Jean that she was able to investigate John's life on location in the USA.

Introduction and editing by Chris Shennan

November 2022

# Summary

## John Shennan

John was the eldest of the family. As such, he had from the beginning a certain status of seniority. Theodore, his youngest brother, tells that during the Bathgate years, when his father retired from the dining room to get ready for church on Sunday, John took his place at the head of the table. His was also the first additional salary coming into the household.

Following Alexander's dismissal from the charge at Bathgate, it was John who took legal advice and remedied the situation, although, sadly, the damage had been done. Later it was John who had to sign his father, overwhelmed by melancholia, into the care of the Crichton Royal Institution in Dumfries.

Although it was known that John had been, for years, seeking a better, perhaps more exciting, life away from Edinburgh, he seems to have reconciled himself, for the time being, to his position as 'head' of the family after his father's committal – living in a succession of rented properties in Edinburgh.

John's escape in 1888 to the Americas – it can surely be thought of as such – came through his employment at the office of the Arizona Copper Company (ACC) of Edinburgh. He had been chief clerk there for a few years. By that time, aged 33, he was a qualified accountant and before he left Scotland was Secretary to the Company.

He went first to the ACC business in Clifton, Arizona. In 1893 he left ACC for a job in Great Falls, Montana. Then, in 1906 he moved to Lima, Peru and finally retired in 1926–7 to Buenos Aires, Argentina.

# John's Early Life

John, the oldest son of the family, aka Jack, was born in Houghton-le-Spring, County Durham, on 7th March 1855. This mining community was where his father, Reverend Alexander Shennan had taken his first charge, as minister of the United Presbyterian Church. John was therefore 11 when the family moved to Bathgate.

John was educated first at an academy in Houghton, followed by the Bathgate Academy and finally two years in Edinburgh. In *The Old Days*, letters to his elder son David, Theodore told an anecdote of John's school days at the Royal High School, which John attended with his younger (by 18 months) brother Willie. Theodore commented:

'John and Willie both went to the Royal High School and John often had to stand up for Willie, who never was strong. Once in the class of mathematics under Munn, who also taught me, Willie had been unjustly punished, and John vehemently objected. Then followed a lively chase of John by Munn over the benches: but I did not learn the ultimate result. My uncle John was the same: he was the fighter in his generation at school.'

Theodore wrote of John's early working life:

'John began his business career in 1871 aged 15 as apprentice to Finlays (*the Edinburgh furniture firm belonging to his maternal great-uncle*) but apparently did not take to it, though it would have been worth his while as, in time, he would have had control of the business, quite a famous one in its time for solid workmanship with capable skilled employees who took a great pride in turning out good work.

John, instead, went over to clerking, bringing him a larger immediate wage but with poorer prospects. Even so, with a decent amount of backbone, he ought to have done better but I'm afraid he was not sufficiently sophisticated.

In fact at that time Finlay's two sons were in their 30s and one took over the business eventually.'

John later described this 'clerking' career:

'My apprenticeship was in the offices of John Waddell Esq. Railway and Public Works Contractor of London and Edinburgh. I was, for nearly seven years, in the service of the Bathgate Foundry Company, situated between Edinburgh and Glasgow where I latterly had full charge of the office. I also made myself thoroughly acquainted, as I had opportunity, with the practical departments of the business – seeing the casting operations – such as retorts for the Paraffin Oil Works at Pumpherston and culverts for carrying off the water at the conjunction of the Tay Bridge at either side.'

During this time, however, John, aged 19, had thoughts of studying medicine. What follows are extracts from a lengthy letter written by his father on 26 July 1877 as a 'Memo to John'. The tone is both chastising and loving as might be expected of a Victorian father and man of the cloth – the lengthy postscript is especially affectionate.

'From the letter enclosed it would seem that you have been consulting strangers in regard to proposed medical study, while you have never given me any distinct intimation of such a wish or purpose. Such being the case, it is no wonder that such purpose has come to naught. During that time, also, you have been consulting others in quite a different direction, thus seeming to show you have no distinct or settled end in view other than a wish to leave your present occupation.

Where you are I doubt not you would find something more

promising opening up to you if you patiently wait for it and are constantly increasing your fitness for it. Fools depend on opportunities and are always hoping for something to turn up, but wise and persevering persons make opportunities and are prepared for them, when they do come by labour and knowledge.

While saying this about the present sphere you occupy, I have not the slightest wish to hinder you if you wish to begin study for a medical life, but if so it must be on proper grounds and with a worthy aim in view. It must not be to be merely in a genteel profession or with the idea it will be an easier or 'jollier' life, or that it will be a surer way of at last and in shorter time gaining a good income. Many able young doctors have to wait long years before they get appointments or openings either at home or abroad. Indeed many of them become almost reckless or desperate on this account, get into low drinking habits and sink into a premature and dishonoured grave. And even when situations are got they are often very unremunerative, there being plenty eager to catch at openings, with little delay, just to see practice.

At the same time, one who embraces the healing profession … cherishes a noble aim. He chooses one of the most difficult, responsible and self-denying of professions and the more successful he is, he must be the more laborious and ready to go thro' perilous and in many cases, most disagreeable and often most trying and repulsive and even harrowing experiences – taking as it were his life in his hands in circumstances where the bravest might quail.

As regards expense, your Mamma and I will not let that stand in the way if other considerations be satisfactory; that expense going on over four to five years at £400 or £500 …Young men after the first year were little or no expense to their parents by getting into inter-sessional appointments and thus gaining experience.

All this implies an enquiry in the first instance, whether your present occupation may not in the end afford an opening as desirable for which your previous training has all along been fitting you. Mr Waddell would surely be able to give you some indication what prospects might be fairly hoped for within the next 8 to 10 years. In no case, whether as in a profession or otherwise, is it to be expected that some sudden leap into a fortune is speedily to be secured. That may often be the case in novels but not in real life.

Your Father

p.s. Whenever you have difficulty or trouble always confide in Father and Mother before any others since none can have the same disinterested aim for your welfare, nor the same gratification in your future success and usefulness that they have. ... This want of outspokenness, confidingness, frankness and the absence of all desire to keep things secret from a father is most unwise and perilous for any young lad. ... When you want advice or help on any of the matters I have referred to, you have only to ask it from me. You must take very special care not to measure your expenses or pleasures by the young men you may meet occasionally as companions ...

Yr Papa

The possibility of a medical career was not taken further. However, over the next four years Alexander did write to various friends and potential patrons asking for advice on his eldest son's 'future occupation'.

In November 1876, John answered a letter from a Mr Gardner of Rugby enquiring about possible openings in a business of sewage and drainage engineering. In November 1878 Alexander replied to a Mr Balfour of Houghton-le-Spring, thanking him for a pamphlet on his business in engineering entitled 'Sanitary Measures'.

**Alexander Shennan's Family, c. 1877**

From L to R: Jean, Lex, Ella, Alexander, Jane, John, Lawson, Theodore, Jessie.

In February 1879 Alexander wrote to Sir William Baillie, Polkernmill, about John, who had been thinking about joining the Civil Service and who had been advised that a 'nomination' or 'presentation' from some influential gentleman 'might assist in opening up a path to a post in Factory Inspection, or the Foreign Office'.

In early 1881, things came to a head when John's mother came across a letter to John from his cousin Willy Knox. In February, Alexander writes a severe epistle to his nephew, Willy, aged 24 (also see Part 4 on The Knox Family):

'I now have a very serious matter to write about. Your Aunt tells me this morning that, by chance or rather by good providence, she came on Saturday morning upon a recent letter from you to our John, in which you speak of some plans of emigrating to America and urge on him all the arguments you can adduce so as to agree to such a plan and set aside any objections he might very naturally feel, as a son and a brother, to such a course.

Apparently too, you write under the view and intention that meanwhile these things should be kept secret from his father and mother and also your own immediate relatives. I need not say how much surprised and displeased I am at such a state of matters. I know John in the end would have told us all about it – but only it might be when too late to withdraw from any rash and unwise steps that had been taken.

Now once and for all it must be distinctly understood I will have nothing clandestine and underhand in any such correspondence. No such plans should have been thought of, far less determined upon without his consulting with us and without you consulting with your nearest relatives. Of course young persons are much disposed to take steps and enter into connexions which they rue only once – but that is through life and He who is wisest tells us that 'he who trusteth in his own heart is a fool'.

Unlike you, John has a good situation and should not lightly throw it up. I daresay if you had been working for 30/- to 40/- or 45/- per week, you would hardly have been thinking of leaving the country 'in the Fall'. Then Jack has no capital to speak of to begin with, in circumstances when all must be outlay for months or even a year or two and I should think he will have too much spirit, either to begin as a common farm labourer with hard work and hard fare – or to begin on your capital and so have a burden round his neck for long. Besides even your capital, now diminishing, cannot be got at when you like. Due notice must be given when it is locked up in bonds. Moreover, neither you nor he have been fitted either in respect of health or former training for the labours and privations of Western life.

I have written plainly because your Aunt and I feel pained by this matter. It would be a mean selfish course not to remember the obligations – vast and beyond payment, you and he are under to your friends who have cared for you and thought and planned for your best interests even.

John does not know I am writing this or that I know anything of your letters and he was quite annoyed and displeased when he learned that your Aunt had seen your letters – all the better that she did – I shall not in the meantime mention but will leave these things to you to do so: it will be better than hearing of them first thro' me.

Hoping you'll aye seek the Higher help we need – and never more than when we neglect to ask it.

I am aye your affectionate Uncle, Alexander Shennan'

In August 1881, John became Chief Bookkeeper and Audit Clerk in Mr Waddell's Head Office in Edinburgh, also assisting in the business correspondence for which he 'learnt Shorthand & had a thorough knowledge of it.' In January 1882, John took lodgings in Edinburgh (although returning to Bathgate for the weekends).

Seeing little prospects for further significant advancement at Waddell's, John started to look again for new employment. Although he had left formal schooling at 15, he had kept up the study of mathematics, and a little French, German and Latin, all with a view to qualifying himself for a position in the Civil Service. He also continued with a decided talent for drawing – having been awarded a prize for that at the Royal High School. He also took a session at the School of Design at the Royal Institution, Edinburgh.

For all the family, Houghton-le-Spring remained a place for holidays: there the older Shennan children had forged friendships that lasted for many years. John was no exception and, in September 1882, his father makes reference:

'We had word from Jack yesterday and as he has not made his appearance in these quarters – he may have gone round to Houghton-le-Spring again, to return hither with his Mamma. He has still a warm side to Houghton-le-Spring.'

In November 1882, John was chosen out of 200 applicants for the Chief Clerkship of the Arizona Copper Company Limited of Edinburgh. The office was in George Street and then Frederick Street, Edinburgh.

'my duties being to superintend the whole Office work, report on same and be responsible to the Managing Director. I may add that during the absence of the Managing Director in America on the business of the Company on two different occasions I have had to take the entire charge of the Office. I have also acted as Secretary to the Company.'

By January 1883, John's father reports:

'Jack has taken up his quarters in Edinburgh again coming on the Saturday and seems to be kept close at his duties. He is studying Commercial Law, Bookkeeping etc preparatory to Examinations as Chartered Accountant. I hope he will get on well.'

In May 1884, however, despite his better position with the Arizona Copper Company, John was still sending out applications for posts, for instance to the Surrey Commercial Dock Company, London for the position of Chief Clerkship at Rotherhithe.

Theodore wrote (in *The Old Days*, letters to his elder son, David, 1940) about one family of friends, the Carrs:

'There were three girls, Alice (my sister Jessie's special friend), Ella and Beatrice. Alice was about Jessie's age, Ella about Lex's and Beatrice was two years older than me.

Ella was the beauty, with lovely dark expressive eyes in a most attractive face. She was very dainty, of medium height with small and fine hands and feet. They were always very nicely dressed and all the accessories were just right. I remember Ella used to wear shoes of what are called I think the monk's type, with a wide heart shaped tongue in front which accentuated the smallness of her high arched feet. I was devoted to her and once brought her shoes to her, while they were with us down at Clynder on the Gareloch. I dropped them quick, for a wasp which was in one of them fastened on my finger and stung me. But I did not much mind as that had saved her from a nasty experience. She had a very small waist, after the fashion of those days, and one of the finest figures I have seen.

After our Jessie's death in 1884, John got engaged to Alice Carr, because she was his favourite sister Jessie's friend, but they were never really in love with one another. Jessie was the bond and after a time it was broken off. That was one of John's mistakes. He should have gone for Ella Carr who was very fond of him and would have stuck to him for life, and what a lovely, attractive wife she would have made.

John had many other nice and physically attractive girl friends, e.g., the Forrests of Glasgow, relations, I think, of our Bathgate friends, the Robertsons. Fine, upstanding, well-educated and, for the time, sophisticated, women and again always well dressed. But he seemed to miss his mark somehow. Perhaps he had too many girl friends, and too few men ditto, though he was quite a man's man for all that.'

In 1885, Alexander (aged 61) was dismissed from his charge in Bathgate after being unjustly accused of inappropriate conduct. Theodore commented:

'John, however, to his everlasting credit, was old enough, 29 or 30, to realise where it would land us all and took legal advice in Edinburgh: the Synod had to publicly recall their judgement.'

As a consequence the family moved into Edinburgh, living in a series of rented homes. Alexander went into a deep melancholic state and was committed to the Crichton Asylum, Dumfries, in January 1887, John signing the papers as 'petitioner'.

By May 1887, John was acting as head of the household.

'11 May 1887: Mrs Shennan encloses cheque granted by Mr John Shennan for £30 in payment of rent of her house at 12 Sylvan Place to 8 June being the final date of the agreement between us.'

Later the family moved on to 23 North Thirlestane Road.

'Friday Morning 20th May

To The Superintendent, High Street Police Office.

Dear Sir

I wish to let you know that a small terrier "Jack" belonging to Mrs Shennan residing at above address, disappeared between one and two o'clock yesterday and we fear he has been stolen or has strayed. He is light brown or liver coloured with white breast and feet and feathered tail & legs, fox shaped head. Some of us will call at your office but meantime I send you

51

this. He will be advertised in today's Evening News & Dispatch, also tomorrow's Scotsman. A reward will be given as he is a great favourite

I remain, Yours faithfully, John Shennan'

In 1888, John did eventually go to the USA. He was 33 years old. Theodore wrote:

'I remember seeing John off to America at the old Caly *(Caledonian Railway)* Station. We were great friends for many years and he did a lot for me to help me through my medical course. Without that help I could not have managed it. I was earning only enough by tutoring to keep myself clothed and to pay occasional fees. I had no bursary and there was no Carnegie Trust in those days.'

Theodore continued:

'Now a letter of John's to show what a different person he was before he went to America. The letter was written while I was a student, and we were living at Thirlestane Road. Evidently the others had gone to Pirnmill on the west side of Arran for the month, and he and I were alone at home. I had made my breakfast and gone off to Arran by an early train. He writes from the Arizona Copper Co's office, at 74 George Street.

3rd May 1888

Dear Theo

After you bolted this morning I had my breakfast. What way did ye no mak a sup parridge? Man, I got awfu' tim *(toom, empty)* aboot 12 o'clock. I've been baad ever sinoe and I'm no to get to Lamlash the nicht and somethings I ordered hevney come and I'm like tae sweer and the Karnarey (anglicised 'Dickie') is at the Johnston's and it's come on rain and Jock's *(the dog)* at the

Hamiltons and I hope to go down the morn at 6.20 but preserve us a its awful sin (*soon*) and I'll have tae take my breakfast the nicht and I'd better no gang tae bed at a' and the best laid plans o' mice an' men gang aft agley and Amen and that a'.

The postman body brocht a scribble frae Mither and she wants me to bring down Jean's gown – a yelly ane but I'm no sure whether its recht or wrang but there's one away by the post this forenoon only I've just sent half of it, the ither, the better half namely the body couldna' be fand – it was absulam absent – I mean.

Mother says their travelling expenses were £1/18/6 – surely this is wrong, it is nearly 13/-each, and if correct how did you manage with only 9/6 or so – like Pat did you take it out in "walkin'"? The wardrobe and all the doors are locked and the keys put under the bell on the lobby table also the front door only it (the key) is not under the bell but here. I won't come up again till Wednesday and will probably return to Lamlash on Thursday for a day or two longer and will see if can't get round to your side of the island.

Love to all, Jack

That's a jolly letter, full of the joy of life. What a change after the nineties began.'

# John in America

## Arizona

John left for America in the autumn of 1888 from Liverpool. He was 33 years old. John sailed on the Cunard Liner, Umbria, leaving on September 1st 1888, arriving in New York on the 10th September. His occupation, as noted on the passenger list, was 'Secretary'. Three days later, John had reported to the Arizona Copper Company's office in Clifton, as an advance of $250 to John Shennan is recorded in the ledgers (held at the library of the University of Tucson) on 13th September.

He went out as an employee of the Arizona Copper Company (ACC) of Edinburgh to a management post in the company's business in Clifton, Arizona Territory. (Arizona was not admitted to the United States until 1912, as the 48th State.)

An advertisement in the *Scotsman* on June 21st 1888 offers Stock and Debentures in the Arizona Copper Company (John Shennan, Secretary). The advertisement states that the Company assets were:

1. Mines and works, including the Coronado Railroad
2. The town of Clifton, with smelting & concentrating plants
3. The Arizona and New Mexico Railroad, extending from Clifton to Lordsburg, New Mexico (distance 70 miles)

The ACC was one of the few successful companies at that time in the southwest copper mining area of the Arizona Territory and New Mexico. The town of Clifton was growing fast and had been linked by rail to the transcontinental Southern Pacific Railroad shortly before John arrived. The general manager of ACC, James Colquhoun, had arrived from Edinburgh in 1883 and had put the mining operations onto a sound footing. Experts had been brought from Scotland to run the new plants, crushing and smelting the abundant lower grade copper oxide ore thus beginning the resurgence of the industry from the earlier days of harvesting the metallic deposits.

It appears (by reference to Railroads of Arizona, Vol III by David Myrick, 1984) that John was involved both in the management of the ACC and the railroad at Clifton. However, he does not seem to have been employed in the Clifton office on the direct management of the mining operations. There is reference to his position as an 'agent' of the company, and there are frequent ledger entries to telegrams sent to John Shennan implying that he was not located in Clifton.

Secondly, it is also shown that payment for a third of his monthly salary came from the New Mexico and Arizona Railroad, built by the ACC earlier in the 1880s to connect Clifton with the transcontinental track at Lordsburg, New Mexico. Clifton, together with developments at Morenci and other places nearby. These towns must have been full of young men ready to work and play hard. The arrival of a new face of relative sophistication from the 'old country' must have made quite a stir.

It is tempting to imagine that the 'manager class' of families coming into that part of the southwestern States would socialise together. Clifton was apparently famous for its dances and social parties. No doubt the arrival of every new young man, especially a single one, would have been met with great excitement among the young ladies.

In Arizona he met and married Alice Nettie James. She was 13 years younger, born June 1st 1869 in Virginia City, Nevada to Isaac Evan James from Marion, Ohio and his wife Charlotte Scholes, from Michigan. Alice's father was superintendent of the Carlisle Gold Mining Company in Virden in New Mexico. On the occasion of the marriage, on 28th October 1889, the engineer, William Polk, decorated his engine assigned to pull the bridal train with bunting and flags.

Alice's elder sister, May, had recently married the local doctor, John Holt Lacy. Dr Lacy features several times in John's marriage: When John was summoned as defendant by the local telegraph company, John Lacy stood as one of his guarantors.

John Holt Lacy came from an interesting East Coast family. He was the youngest child (of 10) of the Reverend Drury Lacy, a pastor of Davidson, North Carolina. Reverend Lacy was prominent in the Confederate cause during the Civil War. Two of his sons served in the Confederate army and, as they died in their early twenties, probably fell in action. John, the youngest child (by a second wife), became a doctor. It seems that there was, at that time – the 1870s – no formal registration system in the American States (as there was in the United Kingdom) for those entering into medical practice. Dr Lacy was based in Clifton in 1890, Duncan in 1900, Solomonville in 1895 and 1910 and at some point at Miami, Arizona, all within a few miles of each other. By the time of his death in about 1940, he was hailed in the local press as a man of some standing in the community.

Theodore, in his letters to his son David, refers to John and Alice living in San Pedro, Arizona. This town could not be located although there is today an area, the Benson/San Pedro Valley which is some 100 miles from Clifton.

It has been difficult to find much to help piece together the day to day life of John and Alice in spite of visits to both Clifton, Arizona and Great Falls, Montana (visits by Jean Shennan). They had two children, both of whom died in early childhood, one in Arizona and one in Montana. This is known only through references in Theodore's letters to John. References to registration of their births or deaths and burials have not been found. Theodore indicates that both children died of diphtheria.

Theodore wrote (in his letters to his son, David) of the first child who died:

'I came across John's letter to Mother on the sudden death of his wee son from Diphtheria in 1893. He had had to leave Alice and Tot in San Pedro to come to Great Falls, on being kicked out of the Arizona Copper Company; and they had been left in the best of health and spirits. He and the kiddie were great chums and played together a lot; and he had this terrible wire when thousands of miles away. You can imagine how broken heartedly he wrote. I couldn't keep the letter; it was too tragic, reminding me too much of my own experience, and I destroyed it. These are the blows that change one's whole life.'

The first child, nicknamed Tod (perhaps christened Theodore – Tod was his sister Ella's pet name for her brother), was of toddler age.

A photograph of Alice shows her to have been a pretty woman – without information to the contrary, it may have been unfair of Theodore to comment in his letters sent to son David that 'John should have married Ella Carr; she would have stood by him ...' It appears that Alice was a loyal wife – four years into her marriage she followed John to Montana after the loss of her first child and then, in 1906, went with him to Peru and later Argentina – thus spending 35 years far from home.

Alice must have despaired at times of John's lack of success in business and his ability to get embroiled in litigations (Arizona), land schemes (Montana) and 'get rich quick' scams (Peru). In contrast, her sister May was in a settled marriage to a professional man and with a family of four.

In all the places John lived after leaving Scotland, he would surely have remained a staunch believer and would have attended the local Presbyterian church (or nearest equivalent) wherever he settled. It has been difficult to find any leads about this in Arizona and Montana.

Theodore's letter above indicates that John was sacked from ACC in 1893. This may have been connected with three pieces of litigation in which John became embroiled during 1892. The following comes from court documents obtained from the Arizona State archives.

In November 1889 in Clifton, shortly after his marriage, John got involved in lending money ($170) to JA Lord, a dentist, on the strength of a promissory note undertaking to repay the loan on demand. As security, Lord gave his dental equipment over to John, which John then allowed Lord to continue using. This would seem like an unusual arrangement.

Almost three years later, presumably after pursuing Lord, who had failed either to repay the loan or to return the dental equipment, John went to court on the matter. Case 324, John Shennan vs JA Lord, was heard at the district court of Graham County at

**The copper mine at Bisbee, Arizona**
Photo by Chris Shennan, June 2018.

Solomonville, Territory of Arizona, on 20th October 1892. Although summoned, Lord, now in Bisbee, another copper mining town in southern Arizona, failed to appear at the court hearing. The Judge awarded John $200 and $38 costs against Lord. There is no indication whether these debts were ever recovered.

As a footnote to this story, the sheriff of Cochise County who received the summons from Graham County and delivered it, in person, to Lord, claimed travelling expenses between Tombstone and Bisbee, for 46 miles at 30 cents per mile (hay and shoes for the horse?).

A little history:

Although copper mineralisation was found by the earliest Spanish explorers of Arizona, the territory was remote and

**The Lyric Theatre in Bisbee Town Centre, Arizona**
Photo by Chris Shennan, June 2018.

copper could not be profitably worked until the completion of the Southern Pacific Railroad in 1876 which made copper broadly economic to mine and ship to market.

By 2011, mining operations in the area were run by the Phelps Dodge Mining Company. This company traces its origins back to 1865 when a US Army patrol, in pursuit of Indians who had stolen some horses, noted strong copper mineralisation on the surface. Five years later a group of ranchers from Silver City, New Mexico, came to the area and claimed areas over the copper mineralisation, hoping to find gold. These areas were later to give rise to the towns of Metcalf and Morenci (Metcalf was named after brothers James and Robert, two of the ranchers; Morenci took its name after the Michigan hometown of a financier, William Church). Church raised $50,000 from the Phelps Dodge Corporation in New York and formed the Detroit Mining Company, with he and Phelps Dodge joint owners of the Morenci property. In 1886, Church sold his half of the company to Phelps Dodge, which built the first copper concentrator in Arizona. In 1882, the Metcalf brothers sold their interests in the Metcalf property to the Arizona Copper Company of Edinburgh, which built a concentrator, leach plant and smelter at Clifton, Arizona.

A depression in the price of copper in 1892 threatened both the Morenci and Metcalf operations. The Detroit Mining Company shut down operations, but the Arizona Copper Company was able to continue because, in 1885, they developed a unique leaching operation that could economically treat tailings from the Clifton concentrator. The leaching operation was further extended to open cast mined oxide-type ores. Ten tons of sulphuric acid per day was provided from an acid plant at the Clifton smelter. By using the combination of smelting and leaching the company was able to survive the economic depression.

To continue with John's story:

In 1891 John again lent money against five promissory notes to a Richard Lakeman; $250 on 18th August 1891, $250 on 20th October 1891, $150 on 30th October 1891, $200 on 14th November 1891 and $200th on 1st December 1891. All loans were to be repaid with interest at 2.5% per month. Repayment was to be at 30 days (the first loan) or 'on demand' for the others. In 1892, John again went to court in Graham County to claim a total of $1280 from Richard Lakeman, who was said to be resident in Saint Louis, Missouri.

In a court document, an 'Undertaking of Attachment', dated 3rd August 1892, two people stood as security for John to the tune of $2400 in the event that the case might be found against him as plaintiff; one of these individuals was his wife's brother-in-law, Dr John H Lacy.

Two days later on 5th August 1892, a 'writ of attachment' was levied against mining claims (Campbell, Tiger, Globe and Pine Tree) near Morenci which were the property of the Defendant, Richard Lakeman.

The case, No 326, was heard on 12th October 1892 in the Graham County Court. The Defendant did not appear, and no plea or defence was offered. John, the plaintiff, was awarded $1322.27 against the defendant with costs of $47. The court ruled that John had a lien (a right to keep another person's property until the owner pays a debt) attached to the mining claims belonging to Lakeman.

It is not clear exactly what happened to these claims but on 21st January 1893 John Shennan is recorded in Tucson, Arizona as having been paid $627 by Richard Lakeman.

In the midst of these ongoing cases as plaintiff, John found himself summoned on 28th May 1892, as defendant in a case, No 331, brought by the Gila Valley Telegraph & Telephone Company (GVTTC). The GVTTC claimed that John owed them $140 being the cost of 14 shares in the company.

On 28th May 1892, the affiant applied for a writ of garnishment against the Arizona Copper Company (ACC) because they believed the ACC had effects in their hands belonging to the defendant. The writ summoned the ACC to answer under oath what, if anything, it was indebted to John Shennan and what effects if any of John Shennan's it had in its possession. On the following day this writ of garnishment was served personally on the President of ACC, James Colquhoun, in Clifton.

On 8th June 1892, James Colquhoun swore before the Clerk of the Court, presumably in Solomonville, to his written answer to the writ of garnishment. He stated that the ACC was indebted to John Shennan in the sum of $294 (his salary), that ACC had no effects of any kind in its possession belonging to John Shennan and that no other person, in the knowledge of ACC was indebted to John or had effects in their possession belonging to him.

John Shennan was summoned to court on 21st June 1892. No judgement is recorded for this case; perhaps John paid up.

Whatever the outcome of this case, as the Arizona Copper Company had become involved and the president, James Colquhoun, must have been somewhat inconvenienced to say the least taking perhaps a day travelling from Clifton to Solomonville to swear to his statement, it is not surprising that John probably was no longer welcomed by his employers and was sacked.

**The Shennan Family in Edinburgh, c. 1895**

From L to R: Lex, Lawson, Ella, Mother (Jane), Theodore, Jean.

# Great Falls, Montana

By 1892, John was already on the lookout for a new post. There is a heading ...

'John Shennan wants position with BA&P' ...

in the president's 1892 files of the Great Northern Railway Company, Great Falls, Montana. BA&P was the Butte, Anaconda & Pacific Railway (Montana) founded in 1892 to carry copper ore from mines at Butte to smelters at Anaconda, although it was also a general carrier of passengers and freight.

John moved to Montana in 1893 although not to the post at BA&P. He and Alice settled in Great Falls where he is listed in the local business directory and gazetteer for 1893 as 'Superintendent' of the Great Falls Iron Works, with a residence at 818 7th Avenue North.

Great Falls had been founded in 1884 and grew slowly until the arrival of the St Paul, Minneapolis & Manitoba Railway in October 1887. By the early 1890s, water power was being harnessed from falls on the Missouri River and mineral smelting operations were under way. Industrial refineries and smelters began operations converting ores containing silver, lead and some gold, mined at Neihart and Barker in the nearby Belt Mountains. Later a copper reduction plant was also operating. Mark Twain in 1895 remarks of the new town:

'Great Falls is one of the prettiest towns in the West, resembling Denver of a few years ago, except that the buildings are finer than those in Denver.'

In July 1894, Theodore wrote to John and Alice:

'It is now a good time since I wrote. I don't hear very much about you. I suppose you are still in America. I believe a letter came a short time ago from you but it was sent off to Mother at Carnoustie, so I have not seen it.

I expect you are in Great Falls now. Have you got rightly started with the business and is that awful strike, which I hope has now its back broken, affecting you much? I hope no for it would be beastly to have such drawbacks just when you have a fine chance of getting on.'

The 'awful strike' may well refer to the Pullman Strike – a nationwide conflict between labour unions and railroads that occurred in the United States in May 1894. This was a wildcat strike by approximately 3000 employees of the Pullman Palace Car Company in response to reductions in wages, bringing rail traffic west of Chicago to a halt.

In the editions of the local Gazetteers between 1896 and 1906, John Shennan appears as manager of the Great Falls Hardware Company at 408–410 Central Avenue with residence at 111 6th Street North. He is also listed as secretary of the Great Falls Ironworks while continuing as manager of the Hardware Company.

The following is from a local publication in about 1900:

> 'The business of the Great Falls Hardware Company was first established by Hotchkiss and Hawkins in 1888, and passed into the hands of the present corporation in 1893, since which time it has been under the management of John Shennan. The store was until recently located at the corner of First Avenue South and Third Street, but is now occupying the new building, erected especially for the purpose, at 408–410 Central Avenue, where they have ample floor and shelf room, covering the entire two floors of the building, each 50 x 100 feet in dimensions.
>
> This is one of the old established business enterprises of Great Falls and needs no introduction to the public. Its commodious salesrooms are stocked with a complete line of heavy hardware, shelf hardware, sporting goods, mechanics' tools,

blacksmiths' supplies, ranchers' supplies, miners' and assayists' supplies, stoves and ranges, tin ware, kitchen utensils and many other lines too numerous to mention here. It has the agency for the California Powder Works, Hercules and black powder, the Waukegan steel barbed wire, and the Universal and Stewart stoves and ranges; also agents for the most approved patterns in hot-air furnaces. This company operates a tin shop, a bicycle repair shop and a plumbing department in connection with the business. The plumbing and repair department is located at 6 Fifth Street South, in the charges of skilled workmen in all branches of steam fitting, plumbing and repair work.'

Another contemporary publication gives information about The Great Falls Ironworks . . .

'The Great Falls Iron Works is the pioneer iron working industry of the north west, having been founded in 1891 during the earliest days of the city by Mr L.S. Woodbury, who has been from its start and is now the president of the company. Commencing in a moderate way, the industry has kept full pace with the growth and development of the state and now occupies four large buildings occupying a full block of land beside outside storage and trackage and steadily employing nearly 100 men, the most of whom are skilled mechanics.

The Great Falls Iron Works makes a speciality of manufacturing mining, milling, concentrating, smelting machinery, and all mining and milling equipment, structural iron, lamp posts, municipal castings, etc. Recently the plant turned out a Trunion center for a 20-foot converter, in a single casting that weighed over 27,000 pounds. The company also carries a full line of steel pulleys, wrought iron and structural steel.

The company does not confine its activities to this city or vicinity, but extends its activities all over the northwest, and its output in various lines, such as lamp posts, manhole plates, ore cars, etc., may be found in almost every city throughout the tributary country. The present manager, Mr C. B. Lockhart, with the able assistance of Miss M.C. Woodbury, the secretary-treasurer of the company and a daughter of the president, and who has been connected in this capacity with the company since its first organization, continually extending the lines of its market territory and popularizing the manufactures of the industry.'

In Feb 1897, Theodore wrote to John including the following:

'I think that I have not written since Alice returned home. It must be very nice to have her and baby back and things must be much more like home now, particularly with such a wonderful baby.

By the way I noticed in the "Scotsman" one day the bare notice that a large Bank in Great Falls had suspended payments. I sincerely hope it has not affected you, when you are beginning to get on so well again.

I am glad you are going to keep Willie Knox *(John's cousin)* where he is. He would just be a humbug if he came to Great Falls and live off you.'

The reference to 'baby' would have been their second child. As with the first child, no record of names, birth or death has been found. The letter suggests that Alice had returned to Arizona for the birth but sadly, however, this infant also died from diphtheria.

Theodore wrote again in May 1897:

'Mr Dougan wrote me last week and is to call this week for some things for Alice and a pair of breeks for you.

An apparition in the shape of Willie Knox from Texas appeared Friday last. He is very thin, rather shabbily put on and fairly done up but still the brisk look he had. He has come over about his aunt's money. He was asking about you and I told him you were all very well but that you hardly ever said anything about business and that in that time there did not seem anything great doing.

If you once let him come there, he is so plausible that he'll sponge on you. I am sorry for him, but still you have others to think of. I must say I would like to know if you are making decent headway.'

In 1899 or 1900 John's mother and sister Ella travelled out to Great Falls. Ella was suffering from tuberculosis and it was presumably thought that the climatic conditions would be healthier for her in the States than in Edinburgh. Theodore went to bring his mother back in 1901. He met his mother and John in Chicago. Ella stayed with John and Alice until the spring of 1905 when she returned to Scotland. In the 1903 and 1904–5 Great Falls Directories 'Miss Ella Shennan' is listed as a boarder at 111 6th Street North.

Ella died shortly after reaching home in Edinburgh. John wrote to Theodore on May 15th 1905 after hearing of her death.

'My Dear Brother

I have your letter of 2nd May and we are so relieved to think that dear little Ella got home sooner than we had expected. And I had pictured her on board the boat, so sick that haemorrhages had begun – and this is one thing she was always so terrified about. She was saved this terrible fear which she often used to talk about. It is very strange that her end should be so similar to Jessie's – she often talked about Jessie.

I am so glad we had Ella here so long – I think it represented four years longer of life to her. For 2 years after she came she seemed to mend until she caught a bad cold and that set the work all back. It was only about a week before she left, she was lying on the sofa in our middle room and I was sitting in my Morris chair reading waiting for supper, when she said

'John, do you think this lung of mine is eventually going to finish me?' I said 'Why Ella should it do so now and not have done so 5 years ago?' 'Well perhaps so,' she said and she brightened right up and we went to the piano and had some music till supper was ready.

It was very strange but on the Saturday and Sunday (6th and 7th May) I felt all the time that something was going to happen and I told Alice so – in fact on the Sunday afternoon I got so restless and nervous that I (Sunday as it was) had to go out into the kitchen and try to get rid of the feeling by doing some work packing and boxing up things (you know we are going to move and give up the house). So when I got your first cable it hardly came as a surprise.

It is going to make a terrible blank in our household because she helped so much around the house – kept my socks, underwear etc in order (you should see some of the darns she did, no-one could ever darn like she did). Then I will never forget what a comfort she was to me a year ago when I was in that terrible fix through the Hardware Company – many a time she was on her knees asking Divine help and guidance for me. I did not see this but I felt it: and how she helped me in copying a lot of lists I had to make up – in fact she always liked to help with the office work.

And she was so proud of the $5 a month she got for Alice Junior's (*Alice Junior refers to Alice's eldest niece, Alice Lacy, who was staying with the Shennans during that time*) music lessons. Dear Girlie her memory will long be kept green. The rumour got abroad here that she had died at sea and everybody was horrorstricken and it was talked about in the streets so we had to put a notice in the paper (The Tribune) to the effect that she was home several days before the end came. The Reverend Mr Crouch, Methodist Church, and the Reverend Mr Agar, Baptist Church, both called – Reverend Mr Ferris,

Congregational Minister spoke to me in the street about it and the Presbyterian Minister was from home in Portland, Ore.

Everybody seems to feel the loss and tender their sympathy.

She and I generally had music and songs every evening – right now lying on the top of the piano is the hymnbook you sent, just as she laid it down – she was very fond of "Sunset and Evening Star" and I sang it the last Sunday night she was here. Also "Face to Face" and "Just for today". It will be a long time before I will feel like singing any more.

Let me know about Dear Mother's health. I hope Ella's going away will not be too hard on her and dear Jean.

With much love my dear Theodore and best wishes a brother can think of – I am aye your affect. Bro John Shennan'

There are other connections between John and Alice Shennan and the Lacys. Some time during the period 1900 to 1905 'young Alice' lived with the Shennans in Great Falls. This was Alice's niece, born in 1890. There is a gap in the children of May between 1895 and 1906 perhaps suggesting there may have been a pregnancy and miscarriage that might have led to young Alice being sent to Montana.

In a letter of Theodore's dated 20th April 1906, reference is made forcibly to 'the Hardware Company':

My Dear John

I have never been satisfied with the accounts I got from my quarter as to the Hardware Company and I went through to Glasgow last Saturday to have an interview with Mr Robertson and get at the ins and outs of the case. If all he tells me is true, it is not a very creditable tale and would indicate that you were not capable of managing the concern. So I should like to have your view of the matters. He told me that he put altogether $15,000 into the concern and he being practically owner, on the basis of 8% per annum on that capital, you to have about $250–300 per month for salary and all profits thereafter to be shared equally between you.

He says he never could get a proper balance sheet out of you, and never could tell how the business was going. He was particularly uneasy as he saw how book debts were growing thinking that you were giving too much credit, in too little security in spite of his incessant warnings not to give credit at all, rather to have the goods lying on the shelves – that his interest gradually got less and less and finally, years ago ceased altogether.

For a long time he got no communication except after a long time a cable – in cipher – asking for more money. Then the gunpowder business and so on. When he sent a man to enquire about the business you were away and someone gave him what information he could. Though the books were not very informing, he seemed to have been sacked as a result of this. Soon after he left, the business went down, as he suggested, because he was really the only one who could manage it. Then he (Mr R.) detailed all the circumstances he knew until in desperation he was forced to put things in the hands of the bank to liquidate. He had come to the conclusion that you were quite incapable of managing a business or even keeping the books.

He got everything paid off and apart from your policy he got about £127 out of it. He would have been even then willing to meet you about the policy, and enable you to keep the benefit of it for your wife, but that some action of you and Alice's determined him to close this up also and he took the surrender value of the policy about $2500 or 2600. He has lost in all about £1500 on the transaction quite apart from not having had the returns he expected.

He did not want to open up the past again, and it is done with, so far as he is concerned, and he still wants to think the best of you, but for my own satisfaction – privately – I should like to know what your aspect of the case is.

He has been much worried over it and has been very ill but is now getting better.

Whatever the truth is, you know now to go cautiously, not to risk your capital and everything else needlessly. So far as I can see you and Alice have lost a great deal of what you had. Do be cautious where you are and be careful not to give any of your bosses a chance of an excuse to think you cannot manage things. Rather concentrate upon one thing and do it very well. Don't start speculating even in certainties.

Now, I had almost decided to say nothing about all this but the interview knocked me down so that my faith is a little shaken.

Now, to leave that, I think one of your duties, now you have a settled income, is to repay Mother the money she lent you, if you can. I don't know how much it is, but the others of us can better afford to stand out.

Love to Alice and you from both of us

Yr Affect. Bro. Theodore S

The reference above, to 'the gunpowder business', may be to a famous disaster in Butte, some 150 miles southwest of Great Falls. Newspapers in the USA reported on 16th and 17th January 1895:

'A fire broke out in the Butte Hardware Company's warehouse near Butte City. There was a large quantity of gunpowder stored in the building and when the Fire Department was fighting the flames the powder exploded killing every fireman except two. This was followed by two further explosions which killed more persons, including policemen and citizens. 43 people were killed and more than 100 were injured.'

It would seem, nevertheless, that the failure of the Hardware Store business led to John's next move – to South America.

However, he left behind another venture in Great Falls.

# Tiger Butte Ranch

In 1903 or thereabouts, John bought a ranch to which the family in Edinburgh contributed substantial funds. The following is pieced together from letters of Theodore's in which he becomes increasingly exasperated with John after the latter left Montana in 1906.

Tiger Butte Ranch, some 30 or so miles from Great Falls, is described as being of some size, and partly at the foot of a hill – Tiger Butte. When the purchase was being considered the following description was sent to Theodore by John:

'The soil is a rich black loam. A good part has been ploughed and there are 60 acres of hay land. Taking everything into account there is enough land to eventually run 500 head of cattle. There is an abundance of timber. There are several places were dams could be built to hold water in the drains and creeks but I think it is quite unnecessary. There are altogether 1280 acres but there are 1000 more acres which we could graze on perpetually and 320 acres we could take up and it forms an ideal stock ranch. There is good hunting and fishing close at hand.'

It had several springs upon it and so always had a good supply of water, even in the driest season. It was partly pastoral and partly pasturage, chiefly the latter. It was considered one of the best ranches in the district in the rain belt and in the driest seasons had plentiful supply of water from springs.

A sketch of the ranch shows the property extending halfway round Tiger Butte. The land was valued in 1904 at $10,000 or £2000 and houses, horses, cattle, machines, crops, fencing, etc. about another £1000. In 'Tiger Butte Recollections' (Library of Great Falls) John Shennan is listed as:

'The Land Patentee and Grantee for the plot area T16N; R6E; Sec 6; dated December 30th 1905.'

Tiger Butte Ranch

To Bird Nest Route
Flint Place
½ mile square
½ mile
320 acres   Barn
Timber
Homestead   2 miles
Cabin
Son's Homestead
Johnson Place   Cabin
Benett Ranch
Cabin
1½ mile
Creek
School Land
Can be rented $5 per annum
320 acres
cabin   Smith Place
Timber
Scoft above Creek

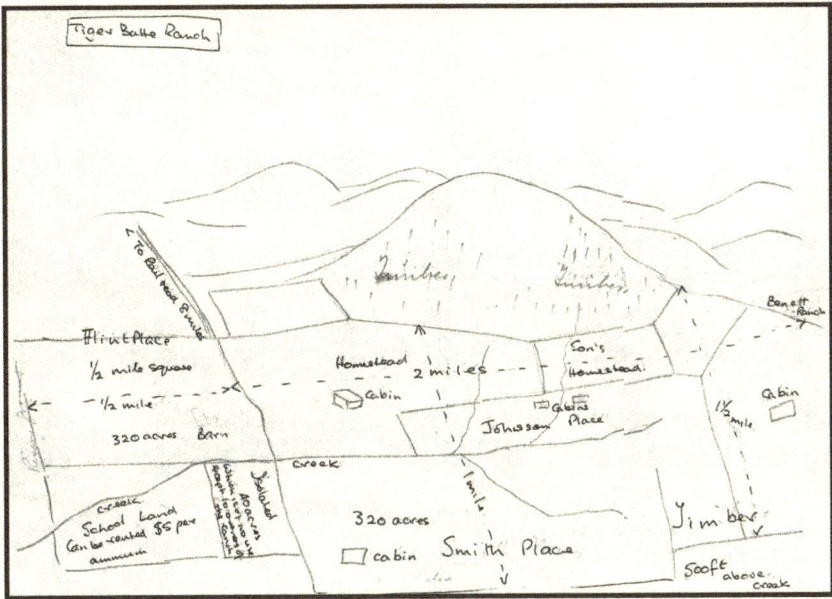

**Jean Shennan's sketch of Tiger Butte Ranch**
C. 2012.

John had urged Theodore:

'if we want to get on to a good thing which will give us all a good return, we would have to send at once, by return, to secure the great deal.'

He thus persuaded Theodore and the other family members in Edinburgh to join with him in this 'investment'. To quote Theodore, 'My brother got me to go into it with him.' Theodore paid £1500; an equivalent sum was contributed by John's mother and brothers, Lawson and Lex. The total purchase was $8380 with a mortgage of $2600 at 7%.

Apparently the original proposal was that John would himself work the ranch, but instead he got in a tenant. Then John went off to South America, leaving the property in the hands of an agent. In the Polk and Ridgley Great Falls Business Directory of 1906,

Alice is listed under the heading of 'Landowners and others living outside of City and receiving mail at Great Falls'.

'Shennan, Alice N, cattle, 1, 6 and 12, 16, 5E, 647 $3,425, care McNair & Skinner.'

In 1908, Theodore takes the initiative and writes to the agent, McNair, in Great Falls asking for advice on sale or rental value of the property. Theodore also asks for help from an old farming friend in East Lothian, Mr Riddell, on the possibility of finding someone willing to go out from Scotland to buy or tenant the ranch.

Theodore tells John, now in Lima Peru, what he is attempting to arrange. John apparently demurs. Theodore wrote ( 8th May 1908):

> 'I have today sent a draft to Mr McNair in Great Falls. I suppose more money into the midden heap.
>
> I think it is hardly fair to say that I am responsible for your being in the ranch. In any case, do you think I would have touched the thing even with the mythical "lang
>
> spune" if I had not been persuaded that you had thorough conviction it was a good thing and trusted you knew it was worth going with.
>
> I cannot see my way to sending more money later. I am enquiring, however, whether there is nothing that can be done over there towards a purchaser or tenant. I sincerely hope that things will improve with you, and that McNair will get rid of that **** ranch.'

In June 1908, Theodore received a reply from Mr McNair. The tenant left in the place since John went to Peru two years before:

> 'has been as bad as possible; all the livestock and personal property has been disposed of and the tenant has not even kept up the hay-ground. Nonetheless McNair is of the opinion that the land is still of value.'

Nothing came of all this: a likely purchaser was, indeed, found through the Scottish contacts but when he went to see the agent McNair:

'He got put off on some pretext or other and went elsewhere and bought a ranch.'

In 1910 (June 10th), Theodore wrote to a Mr Randolph, asking for help in disposing of the ranch. A settlement of $5000 would be acceptable. Theodore mentioned that John's wife Alice was at that time in the United States (c/o Dr Lacey, Solomonsville, Arizona) and could act for her husband if necessary.

In fact, Alice's return on that occasion to the USA is recorded. She arrived in San Francisco in February 1910 on the ship Hermonthis, sailing from Hamburg and Way Ports. Presumably one of the way ports had been Lima. The passenger list tells us she was 38 years of age with four pieces of luggage and was on her way to Arizona.

A final furious letter on 14th December 1911 from Theodore to an unknown addressee, probably McNair, closed the matter:

'Dear Sir

I have heard indirectly that some of the usual curiosities of American or rather United States Justice (?) are taking place with regard to my brother's ranch near Great Falls and that someone or other, without giving my brother, who is in Lima, Peru, any chance of protesting, have foreclosed on the ranch and presumably stolen it. This theft means loss of £1500 which I lent my brother, besides a similar amount lent by my mother and brothers here who can ill afford it.

All I can say is, I wish them all good here and hereafter of their ill-gotten bargain.

No doubt it is part of the plan that I have no chance or time to communicate with my brother to find out the facts of the case.

Yours faithfully

Theodore Shennan'

# John in South America

John went to Peru some time in 1906: in 1908 his address is given as Cerro di Paseo, Lima, Peru.

In 1899, John had been admitted as an associate of the Society of Incorporated Accountants & Auditors. On his certificate, No 4153 dated 27th October 1909, London, 50 Gresham Street, his address is given as:

> 'General Accountant to the Ferrocarril de Guagui (sic) á La Paz, La Paz, Bolivia, South America.'

On John's behalf, Theodore wrote in November 1914 to Mr Paterson of the Society's office in Glasgow:

> 'I have just heard from my brother Mr John Shennan of Lima, Peru and he tells me he has been deprived of his Fellowship of Society of Chartered Accountants evidently through no fault of his own.

> Our constant experience at both ends is of letters going astray and never reaching their destination so that I can quite understand that the letter written by the Secretary of the Society of Incorporated Accountants on May 20th 1911 never reached my brother at all.

> (For return) I enclose the copy of the letter he sent on hearing of his loss of the Fellowship, the decision in June 1913, evidently not having been announced to him or failing to reach him.

> Now there is no doubt whatsoever that he has been engaged in private practice as an accountant in Lima, and my folks have several times recently sent me on letters written on his own office note-paper and referring to work done as an accountant, on his own account.

As you were instrumental in getting him the Fellowship, I know you will be interested in seeing that justice is done him, and I would ask you to do your best in this direction.

His letter will explain things better than I can and will show that, wondering at the lack of communications from the society, he has written to ask why this was so.

I am, Yours Faithfully

Theodore Shennan'

A man away at the end of the earth needs all the encouragement and support from home that can be afforded him.

John was reinstated as a fellow shortly afterwards.

From the yearbooks at the library of the ICAEW (the modern Society of the above) John's movements can be traced using their 'Topographical List – Colonial & Foreign members'.

1910–1914 Accountant Ferro-carril Central del Peru, 606 Calle Coridad, Lima, Peru
1915 c/o Sydney Merritt & Company, Plateros de San Augustin 112, Lima, Peru
1919 Calle Mineria, 189 Altos, Lima, Peru
1920 Avenida del Sol 320, Lima, Peru
1921–25 Paseo Colon 369 Altos (Casilla 1441), Lima, Peru
1926–31 Calle General Urquiza 160, Buenos Aires, Argentina
1932–39 Calle Victoria 2966, Buenos Aires, Argentina

There is a gap of some years before correspondence with John is again recorded. Seven letters from Theodore to John in 1923/24 are about requests from John to Theodore (and sometimes to Alexander/Sandy) for money. The following excerpts give the general flavour:

On 15th January 1923 Theodore wrote:

'Dear John

Yesterday I received a cable from you which I deciphered today as "to avoid litigation and attachment of goods remit by telegraph £75. This matter is urgent." I haven't £75 to spare and the only way I have been able to do is to wire Sandy to ask the lawyer (MacAndrew & Wright) whether he can repay me on realising the consols out of your share. I have back a wire as the affirmation so I instructed my banker to cable you today £75 via London so that expenses are in addition. But what is it all about? Is it that Younger's business? Would you not be better to keep out of these speculations until you see your way clear and have the money to finance them.

I do grudge throwing away money uselessly. I cannot do it and I have been able to help you now only on the condition assured by the lawyer of prompt repayment.

There was £15 or £25 shortly before you left Great Falls, £36 in 1915, £12 in 1915, £10.10 in 1917. All meant to be short-term loans, but I have had nothing repaid and so have considered them bad debts. I am sorry to have to take up this attitude but it is no kindness to you to put you further in debt. If I was well off I should not mind letting you have all you want.

I am glad Alice is able to earn something from her painting and so help with the house; and her niece will also help a bit with her board etc. These things must be a considerable relief.'

At about this time, another daughter of the Lacys, Florence, journeyed out to Lima to live with her aunt for some months. Florence, a stenographer according to her passport application, was 26 years old. Sadly she died a few years after returning to Arizona.

Theodore's replies become increasingly exasperated. On 5th May 1923, he wrote:

'Dear John

I have another cable today "cannot understand telegram, have you sent remittance, very urgent. Unable to raise funds" and also a letter of 17th April. Much against my will and in the teeth of the advice of my banker I have cabled you £35. I grudge it more than I can tell for it means that I will have to limit Min *(Minnie, his wife)* and the boys to that extent plus the £40 sent two months ago. It is too bad. Now this has to be the very last remittance I shall send. I have come to and far past the limit. I realise that it is all going into the pockets of rascals, and I have no money to spare for that. You say you are nearly off your head and tired of it, but it is because of your mistakes in business, and because you trust these damned Peruvians, which should be the last thing in business dealings with them.

I have made up my mind not to remit another penny; and I am not going to receive or decipher another cable. They upset me too much and knock me up.

The exasperating thing too is that all my money remittances have done you no good. It makes me mad to think of it.

Your Affectionate Brother, TS'

In a letter of 17th May 1923, Theodore lists the loans he has made to John and asked:

'Your recent indebtedness to me for sums lent on promises of immediate repayment with interest ...

What can you do about it to secure me any money? Things must be placed on a strict business footing. Not a penny of it all has been acknowledged in a business-like way, except the August 1914 £25 and I should be ashamed if the same could be said of me. You can now understand why not another penny is going down the drain under any circumstantial condition whatever.

By the way I suppose you <u>have</u> given up all your rights in the Great Falls Iron Works and do you get no income from that source? Then have you not some Arizona shares which should be marketable? I think you told me so. Why not make a move about these things?

Forgive my being so hard but you have <u>not</u> been fair to me and have not treated transactions with me in a businesslike manner. Blood relationship is a strong tie, but it can be con-strained.

I hope Alice is well and that things work out.

Your Affectionate brother, TS'

It would seem that Theodore had not had replies for a while and he wrote to the American Consul, Lima, Peru on June 23rd 1924:

'Dear Sir

I should be very glad if you could give me some information regarding my eldest brother John Shennan, Chartered Accountant, as I am not satisfied with such communications as I have had from him. His private address is Paseo Colon 369 Altos.

For some years the principal communication I have had have been cables for money, and several times the disturbing feature has been "to avoid litigation" or "to stop proceedings". It has come to this that I have had to refuse any more cash; because I never have acknowledgement of the sums I send and have had nothing repaid.

Many years ago he was Secretary and then Manager in the USA of the Arizona Copper Company. Thereafter he lived for years in Great Falls Montana before going to Peru in connection with the Cerro de Paseo Mining Co.

Of late years he has, so far as I know, been kept busy at Accountant's work; and ought to be in a comfortable position and certainly not requiring to fear litigation.

So far as I can tell he has always played straight, in spite of very hard luck and he is one of the last I should repeat to do anything shady. He must be somewhere about 68 years of age now and left Scotland for Arizona in 1889 or so somewhere about 32 or 33 years of age.

If he is really hard up through no fault of his own I am willing to help him if I can but I have no great salary had have a family to keep as well as other lame dogs to assist.

I should be much obliged and very grateful of you could give me some light in the matter.'

Some years pass before the following letter was sent to John on 16th March 1932:

'Dear John

I have yours. I am afraid I have the business instinct and consequently write in a business-like way. Not only that but questions like this, even between brothers should be on a strictly business-like footing. For example loans should be repaid to brothers just as conscientiously as to outsiders.

My bankers have just stopped short of telling me I have been a prize idiot and fool to send you anything. It is not been business and it has not been wise. It has not benefited you a scrap, having often gone into the pockets of rascals who have done you in the eye. I cannot fathom how or why you get into these scrapes and it is chronic. Lawson and Sandy *(Lex)* have it too, a want of gumption, and knowledge of the world and the way to tackle people and impress them with the feeling that one has GOT to be considered.

It is all very sad.

Well, I expected a cheque by this time. I have managed somehow to get through these three months, but it has taken some managing.

Well, I hope it is the last time you will write as in your last; and that this is the last time I need to be so straight.

Yr affectionate Brother, TS'

Finally, an explosion from Theodore to his brother Alexander, in October 1938. John has been 'harping on' about the ranch in Montana, about furniture and other items he believed were left to him by his mother (she died in 1914).

'Dear Sandy

John is the sanguineous limit. I am sure Mother left the clock to you, and you have given it to David. I am only giving it house-room, though I have had to get it cleaned. I cannot tell you about Water Stock or Consols and no more money is going to him while he owes me. Tell him with regard to these two, that you have nothing but your old age pension – no, that's wrong. Simply say what you have noted on his letter – I don't know what Aunt Finlay's present was, and it is immaterial.

But he understands, I think now, that I am not paying out one single penny on his account. Send him above, cutting out the first line if you like.

Love from all, Yr affect Bro'

Writing in his letters to David Shennan in 1940, probably having gone over these and other letters that he destroyed, Theodore pondered:

'Thinking back on those happy times (*when John was in Scotland*) makes me wonder if I have been too hard with him during the past 10 or 12 years, and made too much of saving for my family.

During all the nearly 50 years he lived in the Western hemisphere he had misfortune, and he was too honest and simple-minded and kept up his religious instincts instilled during his childhood all his life. But he was not sharp enough and sufficiently alive to his own interests to fight the sharpers and unscrupulous men he met in business; and they did him down in spite of the repeated financial help I gave him.'

John moved in 1926–27 to Buenos Aires and died there in 1939 or 1940 aged 83 or 84. There is nothing to tell how he and Alice lived in Argentina or what their source of income might have been.

Alice returned to Arizona in the autumn of 1940. She died, aged 71, on 18th May 1941, in the town of Miami, Arizona (near Globe). Her death certificate, issued at Miami Inspiration Hospital, states that the cause of death was carcinoma of the uterus, hypostatic pneumonia and respiratory failure.

# PART 3

# The Lawson Family

## C.1800–1919

*By Jean Shennan*

# Introduction

This history is about the family of Jane Lawson who was married to Alexander Shennan. Their youngest child was Theodore Shennan, born in 1869, and who was Jean Shennan's father and Chris' grandfather. He died in 1948.

Introduction and editing by Chris Shennan

November 2022

# Jane Lawson's Parents

Theodore's mother was Jane Steele Lawson, the daughter of Christopher Lawson and Elizabeth Steele.

Elizabeth (Betsy) Steele, born 21st October 1800, was one of the five daughters of John Steele, a toy merchant in Edinburgh. She married Christopher on 13th September 1816 at St Cuthbert's, Edinburgh.

Christopher Lawson was a jeweller and watchmaker in Edinburgh. He was born about 1802. Nothing could be found about his origins, apart from Theodore's comment that the Lawsons may have come from the Lake District. In the Register of Proclamation of his marriage, a John Lawson, Clerk, Princes Street, is named as a witness along with Elizabeth's father. Could this John Lawson have been a brother as he is not, like John Steele, designated as 'Father'.

Christopher's address at marriage is given as 6 Canal Street, Edinburgh and Elizabeth's as 84 Princes Street. By 1828 Christopher and Elizabeth were living with their young family at 7 Hill Square and, between 1830 to 1837, at 25 or 27 St James Square, Edinburgh.

Elizabeth and Christopher had four children: John, Jane, Thomas and Euphemia.

According to information from the British Horological Institute (*Clockmakers and Watchmakers of Scotland 1453–1900* by Donald Whyte, Mayfield Books Ashbourne, 2005) Christopher Lawson is listed with a business address at 19 North Bridge, Edinburgh from 1820 to 1837 and 25 North Bridge in 1834/35 (possibly the same shop if numbers changed). He was in partnership with a Richard Millar until 1825. Christopher was admitted as a freeman of the Incorporation of Hammermen on 5th May 1823, his essay being on watch movements. He paid £100 (presumably Scottish pounds) as entry to the company:

'Edinburgh Evening Courant
4th Feb 1822

Christopher Lawson, 19 North Bridge. Compared and presented a petition craving to be admitted a freeman clock and watchmaker by purchase and the meeting having consented, granted the prayer and appointed as an essay a watch with movement to be produced at next quarter. He paid £50 as the first moiety of his entry money. James Paterson, Landlord. John Bain and James Clark, essaymaster. Admitted freeman in terms as above, 5th May 1823.'

Christopher seems to have been considered a worthy citizen of Edinburgh:

'Caledonian Mercury
Thursday 5th December 1833

Commencing the first Monday of December 1833, Christopher Lawson (Watchmaker, North Bridge) is elected as a Commissioner of Police (along with James Ritchie, Stationer, High Street) for Ward no. 4.'

Elizabeth died on 8th January 1834, aged 34 of dropsy or oedema, probably interpreted today as congestive heart failure due to kidney or heart disease. She was buried in her father's plot, in South Leith Parish Church 'in the S.E. corner of Mr Steele, Toyman's purchase'. Interestingly, in the entry in the burial record she is listed under 'Steele' and the text reads 'spouse of Christopher Lawson, Watchmaker from Dallus's Land, Old Physic Gardens.' These gardens were in the grounds of Trinity College Hospital on the site of the present Platform 11 of Waverley Station, Edinburgh.

By her early death, Elizabeth left Christopher with a young family aged between four and 14: John, born about 1820, Jane

(23rd March 1825), Thomas (21st February 1828) and Euphemia (20th December 1829). Probably the younger children were looked after by the Steele family. In 1834, John, at 14, may well have already been apprenticed to his father. Certainly at the time of the 1841 census, the two girls were living with their Grandfather Steele.

In November 1834 the widower, Christopher, is in trouble. Notices under 'Scotch Sequestration' (equivalent to bankruptcy in Scottish Law) published in *Perry's Bankrupt and Insolvent Gazette*, Saturday 18 October 1834. Similar notices of the same date were posted in the Leeds Intelligencer and the London Gazette:

> 'Lawson, Christopher, Watchmaker, Edinburgh; creditors meet 19th Dec, 2nd Jan at two National Tavern, Edinburgh: claims to be lodged by Aug. 11th: – exam of bkpt. 4th, 18th Dec. eleven, Sheriff's office, Edinburgh – Thomas Brittain Blythe, merchant, Edinburgh, trustee.'

In *Perry's Bankrupt Gazette*, Saturday 31st January 1835, is the following notice:

> 'Lawson, Christopher, watchmaker, Edinburgh; 10th Feb. at one, Royal Exchange, Edinburgh, to receive an offer of composition (a percentage accepted by a bankrupt's creditors in lieu of full payment).'

The catalogue of the National Archives of Scotland lists three items which appear to be matters of litigation between Christopher Lawson and other individuals in 1834 (references CS271 /60720, /74818, /74957.0).

However, according to an advertisement in the *Caledonian Mercury*, Monday 16th February 1835, Christopher Lawson is still in business and also acting as an agent for disposal of goods:

'TO BE DISPOSED OF BY PRIVATE BARGAIN

THE whole EFFECTS of a COAL MERCHANT, who wishes to

retire from the business, consisting of HORSES, CARTS, HARNESS, COUNTING HOUSE and FURNITURE, with the GOODWILL of an established first-rate BUSINESS which may yield from L.200 to L.300 per annum. The premises are well inclosed (sic), extensive, situated in a central part of the New Town, and the business almost daily increasing with customers of the best description, viz who pay ready money.

For farther (sic) particulars apply by letter, post paid, to Mr Christopher Lawson, watchmaker, North Bridge, Edinburgh.

Edinburgh, February 14th, 1835.'

Christopher died on 22nd April 1837 and was buried on 27th April beside his wife at South Leith Parish Church in 'the old South ground, in the northeast corner of Mr Steele, Toyman's, purchase.' The cause of death was recorded as 'Decline' – probably tuberculosis. He was 45.

While Jane Lawson (Theodore Shennan's mother) remained in Edinburgh, John was in London by 1846, Thomas by 1848 and Euphemia by 1856. There is much more information about Jane who was married to Alexander Shennan on 24th April 1855, in *The Old Days*, letters from Theodore Shennan to his elder son, David, 1940.

# John Lawson

The first fact unearthed about John is the record of his marriage on 17th September 1846 at the Parish Church of St James Clerkenwell, to Martha Stewart, of Winchester Street, born in Penrith, Cumbria: her father, John, a builder. John Lawson is identified by reference to 'Father, Christopher Lawson, watchmaker, Edinburgh'.

At a guess John would have been about 26 at the time of his marriage. Calculating John's date of birth from his age as recorded on census returns gives anything between 1820 and 1830. A reasonable estimate would be about 1820, also assuming that he was the eldest of the family. John's profession at the time of his marriage was 'chronometer maker'. He would probably have been apprenticed to his father in Edinburgh. After Christopher died in 1837, John must have come South to London and eventually set up business on his own behalf in Islington.

The Worshipful Company of Clockmakers (a London Guild founded in 1631) does not list a John Lawson as a member. However, the WCC gave the following information (from Britten's *Old Clocks, Watches and their Makers*, 9th edition, London 1986): this book notes entries in London Street Directories for John Lawson from 1845–1887. It seems that he advertised from 1845–53 at 24 Rodney Street, Pentonville, from 1856–58 at 19 York Place and at 355 City Road from 1861–67. He described himself as a watch and chronometer maker.

From the British Horological Institute comes a quote from *Chronometer Makers of the World* by Tony Mercer, 2004. Only one John Lawson is listed:

> 'John Lawson (A -Maker to the Admiralty: M-Manufacturer, finisher and springer), 19 York Place, City Road EC, c. 1840–1859; 355 City Road, 1860–1863; 241 Liverpool Buildings, N, 1883.'

This reference continues:

> 'Blued steel bands. Dial marked with Airy's compensation. Decorative plates. Lawson's auxiliary. Made for G. Gowland, Henessy, Adams, Owen Owens, Sewill, Brockbank and Atkins and Daniels (H&J).'

This is followed by a large number of attributed instrument numbers.

Another internet search found that John placed a notice in the *New York Daily Tribune* of Saturday, May 15th 1852 under the 'Jewellery' section of small adverts:

> 'John Lawson, Chronometer Maker to The Admiralty, No 24 Rodney Street, Pentonville, London – Chronometers supplied, of superior quality, warranted not to alter much on their rates. Pocket Chronometers with isochronal springs. See Greenwich rate paper for 1850–51.'

The census returns between 1851 and 1881 and other sources show that the family of John and Martha Lawson lived at various addresses in Islington:

> 1846 24 Rodney Street, Pentonville (on marriage notice)
> 1840 to 1859 19 York Place, City Road
> 1860 to 1866 355 City Road (possibly the same premises as above)
> 1871 27 Camden Street
> 1876 to 1881 14 Chapel Street, Clerkenwell
> 1883 241 Liverpool Buildings

Some of these places may have been shops or workshops but, no doubt, at that time were all rented premises. They all lie within a half mile radius of the Angel, Islington at the five-way intersection of the City Road (of pop goes the weasel fame), St John Street, Pentonville Road, Liverpool Street and Upper Street.

Of all these properties only 355 City Road exists today; a terraced house dating from the early 1800s or even earlier. It is now a lawyer's office. The Lawsons probably only rented part of the property.

John and Martha had seven children: Edith Jane, Christopher, Caroline Catherine, Agnes, Laura Lydia, John Henry T. and Margaret born at approximately 18-month intervals.

An unexpected event in the life of John Lawson and his family comes from the British Newspaper Archive:

'Reynolds Newspaper
Sunday 27th May 1866
CLERKENWELL
COMMITTAL OF A TICKET OF LEAVE MAN FOR BURGLARY*

Monday, Edward Probert, who refused his address and occupation, and another man who refused his name and occupation, were charged before Mr Barker with burglariously breaking and entering the dwelling house of Mr John Lawson, chronometer maker, 355 City Road. The man Probert is known to the police as a ticket-of-leave (a licence to be at large before expiry of sentence) man and has been twice sentenced to penal servitude, the last time to four years, in 1862.

On Sunday morning at half-past two, the two prisoners were seen to leave the prosecutor's house, and being suspected, were followed and apprehended. It was afterwards ascertained by Mr Inspector Maskell, of the G Division, that the prisoners had broken into the prosecutor's house from the back, having scaled two gates and several walls. The prisoners had turned out all the drawers in the lower part of the house, but all that they had taken away was two pairs of boots, which were found by the police near the spot where the prisoners were stopped.

The prisoners said they had no defence to make, and the prisoner who declined to give his name said his reason for doing so was the great respectability of his parents. Inspector Maskell said he had reason to believe that a previous conviction for felony could be proved against the man who refused his address.

Mr Barker committed the prisoners to the Central Criminal Court for trial.

* Ticket of leave was roughly equivalent to being on parole'

This report was followed a week later:

'Islington Gazette
Friday 1st June 1866
CLERKENWELL – TUESDAY

DARING ESCAPE FROM A POLICE VAN. – Robert Probert, who said he was a shoemaker, and who gave a false address, and a man who refused both his name and address, were charged before Mr Barker with burglariously breaking and entering the dwelling house of Mr John Lawson, Admiralty chronometer maker, 355 City Road, and stealing therein two pairs of boots, etc.

Mr Ricketts, solicitor, defended the prisoners.

The evidence went to show that on the morning of Sunday, the 20th inst., Police Constable Few, 174N, saw the prisoners leave the prosecutor's house, and suspecting that they were up to no good, followed them. Seeing Inspector Maskell of the G Division approaching, he called upon him to stop them, but this was not done until after a smart chase and a most desperate resistance on the part of the prisoners, and it was with great difficulty that they could be got to the police station.

It was afterwards found that the prisoners had gained admission to the prosecutor's house by scaling several low walls at the back and breaking the shutters. When in the house they had ransacked all the drawers in the lower rooms, but had taken away only two pairs of boots, which were found near the spot where the police intervened. The prisoners had been remanded to enable the police to make enquiries as to their antecedents.

Today the prisoners were brought from the House of Detention in the police van, and on arriving at the court, instead of the van being driven into to the courtyard and the gates closed, as is the usual wont, the prisoners were handed out of the van in the public road to be taken through the police station. When Probert was released from his cell in the van he jumped on to the step, and instead of quietly allowing himself to be handed by the police, he rushed into the crowd that had of course assembled to see the prisoners get out, and made his escape, upsetting a butcher boy with his tray of meat in his flight. He was quickly pursued by the police, but it was not until he had traversed nearly half a mile that he was captured and brought back, when he was handed over to the safekeeping of Turner, the Gaoler.

Inspector Maskell, G Division, reminded the magistrate that on the previous examination of the prisoners, the prisoner who refused both his name and address, said he did so on account of the respectability not only of his parents but of himself. He had since ascertained that his name is Joseph Pulley, and that he had only been liberated a few days from prison, having suffered three years' penal servitude on a charge of felony. He also understood that previous to that sentence he had been in the House of Correction on a similar charge.

Police Constable Newbould, 151N, said that Probert had been sentenced to three months' imprisonment, 12 months' imprisonment, and twice to three years' penal servitude, all the sentences being for charge of felony. He never did any work, and in addition to his being an idle, dissolute fellow, he was the companion of most notorious thieves, burglars and prostitutes.

The prisoners, who laughed whilst their antecedents were being related to the magistrates, said they should reserve their defence to a higher tribunal, where they had no doubt they would have full and ample justice done them. However, if the magistrate pleased, he could settle the case at once, and thus save time and expense. Mr Barker committed the prisoners to the Central Criminal Court for trial on the charge of burglary.

The prisoners danced out of the dock, and treated the whole proceedings as a good joke.'

A 'prequel' to the above is the following report:

'The Morning Chronicle

Wednesday 15th July 1857

Alfred Smith, 15, and Edward Probert, 14, were sentenced to three months' hard labour for stealing a silk handkerchief, the property of Mr W.H. Allen of No 15 Anetty Crescent, Islington.'

John Lawson's business was not wholly successful. In the London Gazette of November 22nd 1867, p. 6293, there is a notice of the Court of Bankruptcy of a deed, dated 30th October 1867, the debtor being one John Lawson:

'Late of 355 City Road, now of 17 Liverpool Terrace, Liverpool Road, Islington, Middlesex, chronometer maker. The nature of the Deed ... where you, the debtor agrees to pay all his creditors a composition of five shillings to the pound within six months from the due of the Deed.'

At Christmastime in 1875, Jane Shennan, following her Aunt Finlay's death on the 10th December, sent a parcel of clothing to her brother John Lawson in London. No doubt she knew that his business was not doing so well and that his large family, aged from 15 to 26, might be in need of some help. The following indignant letter written by Alexander to his brother-in-law on Jane's behalf, explains what had then happened:

'5th January 1876
To John Lawson
11 Chapel St, Islington

Sir

On reaching home from Edinburgh this afternoon my wife
handed me the strange and, I may say, unnatural ... which
you *(rest of sentence illegible)*

In our connexion here we regard it as quite an ordinary thing
for brothers and sisters and their families, to do and give in
the way of mutual obligation, what would not be admissible
with strangers, and with this view of things it was quite in
kindness and good faith that Mrs Shennan sent what you call
the "rags" she forwarded, thinking that what she could not
well wear, as all about us know of us being in mourning attire
on account of Aunty's death – might yet be of use to some of
your young folks. As for their being "rags", they were chiefly
what Mrs S had been wearing, and would still have worn for
her Winter and Spring attire, and we certainly had not the
idea, that what would be good and respectable clothing for
persons in our position, would only be as "rags" for you.

I can't understand what jaundiced ideas have got possession
of your mind, when you ascribe your sister's kindness, to her
wish to insult you or yours. I think Edith will tell you whether
she was not a favourite with her Uncle, rather than otherwise,
strong affectionate interest in her was shown in regarding her,
as I would do still, if she were here, just as one of the family.
So when you talk of being insulted by the clothing been sent
and ordering them to be returned, and of surely being
thought a "spiritless creature" were you to agree to accept
them, I do think the less of that tone you express, the better!
If <u>you</u> forget, <u>I do not</u>, how I sent you my deceased sister's
Gold Chain and other things towards the price of a G. Watch,
– and I have never since received them back, or any

equivalent, further than that you returned some silver studs, that were of no value to you.

Then the loan of £25 which I was to receive in a few months again – principal and interest – unpaid. In deference to your sister's wish, I had intended to say nothing further about that claim – however the spirit of your letter is such that I must remind you, there will, ere long, be payments from "Steele's Trust" which will enable you to prove your <u>honourable</u> and <u>independent</u> spirit of <u>repaying me,</u> as well as others, who have lent you monies at different times.

I am sorry to have to write these things as I had expected that matters might yet be in such a state between our families as to admit of future kindly intercourse, but when you take up the role of one indignant and aggrieved and even insulted, it is well you should hear something on the other side and see it is <u>you</u> and not me, who have been <u>insulting</u> and that it is <u>we</u> and not you who have the right to complain of being ill-used.

I am, Sir,

Yours faithfully, Alex Shennan'

Martha, John Lawson's wife, must have replied immediately as Alexander writes to her in a more conciliatory mood a few days later:

'11th Jan 1876
To Mrs Lawson, London

Dear Sister Martha

Mrs Shennan received your kind and judicious letter and you may be sure we don't blame you or Edith in connexion with the curt note sent by John. I certainly did feel greatly annoyed that what Jane had intended in all kindness, should have met with such a contemptuous reception as his words implied and indeed expressed. Simply addressed to "<u>Mrs Shennan</u>" without any indication of courtesy, far less of brotherly feeling, it quite conveyed the idea that he would have flung back the gift, meant in kindness with utter loathing and scorn.

However, on reading your letter, it would seem that he really had severe illness on him when he wrote in such terms and that he was hardly in a state to judge wisely of what his words implied. In the circumstances, I think (and Jane agrees in this) that it will be better on the whole just to regard my (last) former letter as unwritten and that you had best just destroy it without minding to show it to John.

I can assure you Jane always retains very kind and affectionate feelings towards you and your family and also for John, tho' he seems to cherish almost antipathy towards her – being so ready always to put the worst construction on what she says and does. But there's no use dwelling in that; we hope he may soon be thor'ly recovered of his serious illness and that all good – present and to come – may be your portion. We heard from Mrs Shovlar of Edith's having been unwell, but were glad she could also tell us she was feeling better in health.

With loving remembrances then from Jane and self to you and yours,

Yours Truly, Alexander Shennan'

Later, in 1878, Alexander Shennan had correspondence concerning John Lawson and the Steele Trust – the trust by which the Lawson's grandfather, John Steele, left his money for his daughters and their children. It appears that John felt that he had not had full settlement of any entitlement and had made a claim against the trust. Alexander writes on June 7th 1878 to the solicitors in Edinburgh (McAndrew & Wright) who administered the trust:

'You will see that Mr Lawson still keeps by the sing-song of ill-feeling against him and being unnecessarily kept out of his means – of course if he will keep harping on that string instead of feeling himself wholly to blame – and his agents – in the matter, he must just be left to indulge that fancy.'

In a later letter dated 6th September 1878, Alexander ends as follows:

'nor can J.L. expect us to saddle ourselves with responsibilities which he alone will reap the benefit. I've lost enough to him already and with little thanks.'

Alexander at this time was also writing to his niece, Edith Abbott, John Lawson's eldest daughter, now married. It would appear that she had been supporting her father's case on the matter:

'4th September 1878
To Mrs Abbott, London

My Dear Edith

We have been staying at the seaside for a time, and only returned the night before last – your letter had come here and been sent on to Portobello and had to be readdressed hither, so that has abused delay in receiving your note and answering it.

I must just repeat what I have said again and again, that I am anxious to have your father's money matters settled as soon and as satisfactorily as possible. I observe what Mr Gibson has written your Pa, seeming to convey the idea that he has been anxious to have the matter settled and expense saved and that I have been standing in the way. I don't understand that at all and intend asking Mr G to explain it. He has done nothing in the matter toward expediting things which I have in any respect of him; like myself he wished ... (illegible) ... provided there shall be no delay on my part to have matters settled.

There are several statements in your father's memorandum I must refer to shortly. For instance he harps on the old thing about a little goodwill on the part of the Trustees obviating the expenses he has been at and still purposes incurring as against Mrs Butler *(Thomas Lawson's widow)* – surely a little common sense would suggest that we as Trustees could do nothing in the case when the money was arrested in our hands – until he furnished us with proper evidence that she really had no claim on him – and as for any want of "goodwill" he should have been the last to complain of any lack of evidence of that on our part. The evidence has been of long standing.

Then he says Mr McAndrew "either did pay or was ready to pay" his share in Feb '77 on <u>McAndrew giving a guarantee that Mrs B's claim was settled</u>, but your father himself "repudiated the whole affair and paid the costs". So he admits thro' some feeling of pride or stubbornness he prevented our receiving a sufficient guarantee for paying him his money in Feb '77 – and yet at this date will persist in speaking of <u>our want of goodwill</u> being the hindrance.

Then Mr L. speaks of an action his Agent is about to bring against Mrs B – hitherto one difficulty in securing (compulsorily if need be) her consent to the arrestments being removed has been that her address could not be got – the quotation I have just made about the contemplated "action" seems to indicate that difficulty is now out of the way, why cannot your father have that legal procedure hastened as much as possible so as to remove all difficulty our Law Agents have in the matter. For my part, when delay is only causing me further <u>trouble and expense</u>, I should be only too glad if the money were sent off at earliest possible date. Same time your father cannot expect that we should take upon ourselves <u>new</u> money responsibilities to relieve <u>him</u> of risks and remove delay for which he has only himself and his agents to blame . . .

Having much to do after reaching home and my work being in arrears, I shall not prolong this letter, nor refer more particularly to the other points in your letter but I'll not lose sight of them – I'll endeavour to manage a Carte if I can lay my hands on a copy – so glad to find you are so happy and comfortable in your married life. Of course your experience as Uncle's "Housekeeper" (!) for a time would be part of your training for that!

No more at present but all affectionate remembrances and good wishes from Uncle Shennan'

John and Martha Lawson's eldest child, Edith Jane, married a widower, Henry Abbott, in Islington in 1878. In the 1881 census return they were recorded living in 2 Redfern Villas, Tottenham. Henry's occupation was given as 'Clock Dial Engraver' and his 17-year-old son, Henry, as 'Heraldic Engraver'. Edith's child of the marriage, Frederick, was 2 months old. Edith died young, aged 38, in 1886.

By the time of the 1891 census, Martha Lawson was living as a widow 'on own means' with her two youngest daughters both now in their 30s, their occupations being 'dressmaker' and 'mantle maker'. In 1901 she was 80, at 144 Seven Sisters Road with her unmarried daughters, Laura and Margaret, both dressmakers, and Agnes, housekeeper. The household also included Martha's grandson Frederick Abbott, aged 19, an engraver.

# Thomas Lawson

Thomas Lawson was born on 21st February 1828, his birth registered in the District of St Cuthbert's, Edinburgh by Christopher Lawson, watchmaker.

'Tom' was, according to Theodore, Jane's favourite brother. He seems to have followed John to London. He writes from there to Jane in October 1848, soon after arriving:

'31st October 1848, London

Dear Sister

I regrett (sic) to think that John's not writing you should lead you to suppose that I have not agreed to the proposal of the Trustees, to transfer £50 of my share to my brother, rather as have it from his own and thereby create a misunderstanding among the others.

John sent me under cover your letter to him respecting it accompanied with a request to agree to it. I no sooner read your letter and his note than I wrote him an answer by return of Post – and at the same time a letter to Mr McAndrew – signifying to both my willing consent. About twelve days ago I received an acknowledgement of my letter from Mr McA in which he said that he would lay it – together with another from John before the next meeting of the Trustees and that he would write again after the meeting takes place and tell me the result. I am glad that I have it in my power to do him the service.

Mr and Mrs Tulloch & also Miss McGillivray are keeping well. Little Johnny is not much better. John and Martha are in good health – Totty is getting quite strong – she can walk well and I think a more intelligent child at her age there is not.

I have not gone out to Cheshunt yet to spend a Sunday with Mr Balgarnie but I will either the first or the following Sunday take that pleasure.

I hear that cholera is assuming rather a serious appearance in Edinburgh – there are very few cases of it in London.

I am keeping well & getting on well. Give my love to Euphemia and hand my compliments to my Uncle and Aunt and Mr and Mrs Gibson. I am glad to hear you have got your trunk safe and sound.

I remain your affectionate Brother, Thomas Lawson'

There was a serious cholera outbreak in 1848/49 in London and again in 1853. In 1854, the famous early example of epidemiological research led Dr John Snow to identify that the source of infection in a specific area of Soho was the water supply from the Parish Pump and not the 'foul miasma' hitherto blamed for the infection. This led, of course, eventually to the building of the London Sewer System designed by Bazalgette.

Totty is likely to have been Edith, John Lawson's first child who would have been about 14 or 16 months old. It can be speculated as to whether Thomas was helping John with the money because John was still establishing himself in business; and did Jane lend Thomas her trunk for his goods when he went to London? The letter also shows that there was a firm network of friends and acquaintances from Edinburgh, already settled in London.

Thomas married Mary Smith on 25th July 1859 at St John's Church, Paddington. Thomas's occupation is given as 'commercial clerk' and confirmation of identity is given by the recording of Christopher Lawson, watchmaker, as his father on the marriage certificate. Mary Smith's father, Thomas Richard Smith, was a gardener. The address given for the couple is Star Street.

They appear in the 1861 census living at 147 Princes Street in Lambeth St Mary Parish. Thomas, aged 29, with birthplace given as Scotland; Mary, aged 24, as Uxbridge. This is more than likely to be the correct couple. The occupation of Thomas is given as Brass Foundry Clerk.

They seem to have had a son, called Thomas Christopher Lawson, born on 30th March 1862. Sadly, however, the record is followed by the child's burial, aged 14 months, on 27th February 1863, in Norwood Cemetery, Lambeth. The family address then was Tower Street, Westminster Road.

Thomas Lawson died at some time between 1861 and 1864. There are records (Ancestry.com) for five individuals named Thomas Lawson dying in their early 30s in London in those years. One died in July 1861, aged 30, and was buried in Norwood Cemetery. If this is the correct Thomas and the parent of the baby that died, the child would have been just newly conceived.

From Alexander Shennan's letters we learn that Thomas's widow remarried. There is a marriage record on 26th July 1864 for a Mary Lawson, widow and James Butler, Coachsmith, both of Judd Street, at St Pancras Church, St Pancras Parish. Her father's name is given as Thomas James Smith.

The Butlers appear without children in the 1871 census, living at 1 Gee Street, St Pancras.

In Edinburgh, the business of the Steele Trust was further complicated by a claim from Thomas Lawson's widow, Mrs Butler, although only passing reference is made to that in Alexander's correspondence.

# Euphemia Lawson

Jane's younger sister, Euphemia, was born in December 1829, her birth registered in the St Cuthbert's district of Edinburgh by Christopher Lawson.

After their mother's early death in 1834 followed by the death of their father three years later, Euphemia and her elder sister Jane went to live with their Aunt Jane and Grandfather Steele at 2 South St David Street. In the census for 1851 Euphemia is living in the Steele household, aged 20, occupation governess.

Five years later in 1856 she is in London. Was the move perhaps because her sister Jane had been married the year before and had moved to County Durham? As Grandfather Steele had died in 1846, the household at 2 South St (David Street?) was now that of John Finlay, married in 1845 to John Steele's remaining unmarried daughter, Jane.

Euphemia's brother John had made a home for her in Islington as she was married from 19 York Place there. The wedding took place on 3rd April 1856 in the Parish of St Mary, Islington to Alexander Smith, a teacher of pianoforte, of 23 Dame Street, Islington, son of Alexander Smith, clerk. One witness for the marriage was John Lawson.

Within 10 years she was widowed. On 8th April 1867, aged 37, she remarried – in the parish of St George the Martyr, Battersea. Her new husband was William Shovlar, from Meopham in Kent, aged 40, a widower with two children and a bootmaker to trade. Their address was 9 Gladstone Street, Lambeth. The surname is also spelled Shovelar or Shoolar. William was employed in an 'Army Clothing Department'.

It would seem that money was short as the Shovlars received a loan of £5 from Alexander Shennan. He sent half a Bank of England

£5 note (serial number and date of issue recorded) on 30th July 1867 with a promissory note to be completed and returned by Euphemia and William. On due receipt of this, promising repayment within six months, Alexander sent off the other half of the bank note on 1st August 1867. However, after 10 months, Alexander writes to William Shovler:

'8th June 1868
To Mr Shovlar, 31 Miles Str, South Lambeth

Sir

I have been much surprised and annoyed at the fact that you have allowed the £5 I lent you to stand still unpaid. Several times I have thought of writing to you at the Army Clothing Department, but now I would simply ask you to return the money lent you without delay – not later at all events than the next 5 or 10 days – I need the money now and when I put myself about to make you the advance for six months, you should have made some acknowledgement of the kindness by prompt repayment to a day – instead of that it is now about ten months since you received the money. This matter must have your immediate attention.

Yours, – as you conduct yourself – Alex Shennan'

In the 1871 census the Shovlars are living at 12 Pensbury Street, Wandsworth with Euphemia's two stepchildren, William 11 and Annie 9.

In 1876 Alexander writes somewhat tersely to Euphemia after she seems to have made a claim to some inheritance following her aunt's (Aunt Finlay) death in December 1875: there is a sting in the tail!

'24th August 1876
To Mrs Shovlar
27 Pensbury Street, Wandsworth Road, London.

Mrs Shovlar should be better informed in regard to matters ere she writes in the terms she has done to my wife, Mrs Shennan. Though a Trustee on the late Mr Steele's Trust, I am not a Trustee on the late Mrs Wm Findlay's Trust. She left her property under Trusteeship of her husband and his son John Findlay who is now the sole surviving trustee.

The whole residue of her estate, lying monies, furniture, bed and table linen, silver, china etc were all left to Mr Findlay, with the exception of Legacies of £50 each to Mrs Shennan and James and John Findlay. Wearing apparel and trinkets also coming to Mrs S – and other items after Mr Finlay's life rent of them. Among other things included in the residue were certain loans, the acknowledgements for which were found in her repositories after her death and one of them was from you with signature and stamp, intimating the loan from your Aunt – the amount being from £7 to £10 – if my memory serves me right.

Since Mr Findlay's death these documents belong to John Findlay as one of his father's representatives and if he, as you put it, "instructs parties to write (you) on the plea that you owed your late Aunt money" that is a thing with which I, as one of Mr Steele's Trustees have nothing whatever to do – and hence your remarks as to being hurt "that after getting the bulk of the property any of (us) wish to take any out of your small share" is as groundless as it is unbecoming and uncalled for.

While writing on this subject, I have lying before me the Promissory Note for £5 lent you several years ago and signed by your husband and yourself. Certainly you cannot complain of my being hard or exacting during these years and

I now ask for an <u>early</u> settlement and repayment so as to avoid any further trouble and expense.

Alex Shennan'

By the time of the 1881 census, the Shovlars are living at 137 Eversleigh Road, Battersea without family.

Euphemia died in Lambeth in 1892, aged 63. The birth of her stepson, William Wilson Shovlar, was registered in the census of the third quarter of 1860, in the registration district of St Olave, Southwark. In 1883 his marriage is registered in the second quarter of 1883 in the district of St George, Hanover Square. By 1911 he is widowed, listed as a visitor at 15a Grafton Street, Bond Street in the above district: his occupation 'packer, jewellers'. He died in December 1919 aged 59.

PART 4

# The Knox Family
## C.1847–1910

*By Jean Shennan*

# Introduction

This history is about the family of Alexander Shennan's sister, Christina Graham Shennan. Christina was married on 14th September 1847, aged 32, to William Knox, aged 37.

The focus is especially on the Knox family and their life in what was then British Guiana (modern day Guyana), and their subsequent return to Great Britain. This link with South America was of particular interest to Jean and she visited Georgetown in Guyana on a Caribbean holiday.

Theodore Shennan, born in 1869, was Alexander Shennan's youngest son and was Jean Shennan's father and Chris' grandfather. He died in 1948.

Introduction and editing by Chris Shennan

November 2022

# Christina Shennan and William Knox

Alexander Shennan's sister, Christina Graham Shennan, was born on 23rd August 1815. On 14th September 1847, aged 32, she married William Knox (born 13th March 1810). Both of them belonged to Edinburgh. Christina's address is given as 20 Haddington Place. The ceremony took place in St Mary's Church, St Cuthbert's Parish.

William Knox was the eldest son of Arthur Knox, a glazier, and his wife Jean Roper. He had three brothers, George, Arthur and John, and two sisters, Katherine and Janet. The children were born between 1807 and 1821 in the Edinburgh parish of St Cuthbert's. Their father Arthur, died of 'apoplexy' (probably a stroke) in 1833 aged 33 but Jean, their mother, lived on into her 70s. The family lived at 16 Barony Street, Broughton in Edinburgh's 'New Town'. This house (or flat) was owned by the Knox family as it was later referred to as being the property of William Knox.

William Knox and Christina Shennan would, therefore, have been near neighbours and certainly members of the Broughton United Presbyterian Church. According to Theodore Shennan's cousin, Hay Shennan, William Knox was a great friend of Christina's eldest brother, John. William, like his deceased father Arthur, was a glazier – so a connection between him and John Shennan, the builder, is not surprising.

As an aside, it is interesting how relatively 'old' many of these women of the family were on their marriage in the mid-1800s. Perhaps it was purely a matter of economics – a young couple had to wait until the prospective husband was earning enough to support a family before they would marry. Christina and William were of a similar age but William had already been working to establish himself in the overseas colony of British Guiana.

115

British Guiana (present-day Guyana) – sandwiched between Suriname and Venezuela on the North East Atlantic coast of South America – was originally settled by the Dutch at the beginning of the 17th century. During the French Revolutionary War, because Holland was then occupied by the French, Guiana was fair game. It was captured by the British in 1796 and returned to Dutch control in 1802. During the Napoleonic War that followed, Dutch Guiana was again taken by British Forces in 1813 and officially ceded to the UK in 1814 by the Anglo-Dutch Treaty.

Demerara was one of three former Dutch colonies (the others were Berbice and Essequira) which were consolidated in 1831 under British rule as British Guiana. Georgetown, the main port of Demerara, was made the capital of the colony. For a long time the British continued the Dutch colonial government ways including their legal system.

From the late 1700s there was a considerable Scottish community in Demerara; for instance, many plantations were run by Scots from Inverness and Moray.

British Guiana was considered as part of the West Indies and, until the 1880s, its economy was completely dominated by sugar cane production. The plantations were dependent on slave labour until the 1830s – the final abolition of slavery there being in 1838. As slavery was phased out, labour was provided through immigration from Portugal (mainly from Madeira), Malta, Germany, India and the West Indies. These people came as indentured labourers to the plantations. Only the Indians and West Indians were of much use for field work: the others suffered terribly from tropical diseases, drank excessively or drifted into more profitable occupations. Many Indians and Portuguese eventually returned home with substantial savings. The Portuguese particularly would quit the plantations upon expiry of their indentures and go into some sort of small business.'

By the time of his marriage, William was already in business on Main Street, Georgetown (British Guiana) as a house painter and decorator and general merchant of household fittings, in partnership with a Mr Morison.

From the diaries (1843–1868) of John Thomas Hynes, Catholic Bishop of British Guiana:

'Sept 1846. Morison & Knox commenced painting the church – Contract $750.' (*The currency was the Spanish dollar or 'piece of eight'.*)

It would appear that William returned in 1847 from Edinburgh with his bride to an established place in the growing community of entrepreneurs, tradespeople and professional folk who were building a colonial life in British Guiana.

As Morison and Knox, and later (March 1857) as 'Wm Knox – late Morison & Knox', the business was catering for the outfitting and decoration of homes and also selling materials for the leisure pursuits of watercolour and oil painting.

Christina and William had three children. Margaret was born on 30th November 1851, Jeannie on 7th May 1855 and William Arthur on 9th March 1857. The gap of three and a half years between Margaret and Jeannie may indicate the loss of a child.

Nothing specific is known of their family life in Georgetown. Living in British Guiana, in spite of the risks of the transatlantic voyage and of tropical disease once there, did not seem to put people off from colonisation and hope of advancement and prosperity.

Certainly, by May 1851, William was well established, as an advertisement transcribed from a local newspaper proclaims:

Royal Gazette May 29th 1851

Morison and Knox.
Beg to draw the attention of their friends and the public to several large lots of
HANGING PAPERS
now opening and which will be disposed of very low for cash
A LOT OF REMNANTS, CHEAP

GILT PICTURE MOULDING
Flat and rabbetted
One new and one second hand FLOOR CLOTH
And a choice selection of
PASSAGE CLOTHS
Floor cloths to order at various prices

A very complete assortment of articles required in the
PAINTING AND GLAZING TRADES

Artists' Colours and Materials

WINDOW AND PICTURE GLASS– THICK PLATE for glass Cases, etc
Fluted, coloured and ground glass

Paint and Lamp Oils–turpentine and varnishes
VENETIAN BLINDS
Ditto made up to any size or any colour–ladders and cord

Six large second hand Gallery blinds, in very good order for sale

M&K beg to announce that arrangements have been made for them for
RE-SILVERING OLD LOOKING GLASSES or SUPPLYING NEW ONES.
Orders for which will be punctually attended to.

No ladders etc will be hired, except as written-applications from respectable and responsible parties, and will be charged for according to the time they are kept.

Old Court House

The colony appears to have been well supplied by shipping lines. One newspaper of Georgetown, the *Royal Gazette*, lists several vessels each week arriving and departing for destinations in Europe and the USA. Shipping from the UK came from Glasgow, Liverpool, Bristol and other ports, supplying the colony and bringing passengers to and from. Various references in Alexander Shennan's letters show that friends and acquaintances travelled between British Guiana and Scotland bringing news.

Letters travelled via the West India Mail Service: in 1841, for example, out mails left Southampton on the 1st and 15th of each month, travelling via Corunna and Madeira to St Thomas in the Virgin Islands, reaching there in 19 days. From St Thomas the mails were forwarded in four different steamers, that to Demerara making a total of 27 days and fifteen hours from England.

Glancing through the Georgetown Gazette between the 1840s to the 1870s the expansion of Georgetown 'society' and its cultural aspirations can be seen: parties, horse racing, theatre and a concert hall.

Description of Georgetown, written in 1850, as part of an account of the most recent yellow Fever epidemic of British Guiana

'Georgetown, the capital, is situated at the mouth of the Demerara river. It is a large town, composed of wooden houses, laid out in wide rectangular streets. The houses are raised from the ground on pillars, and are, for the most part, roomy and well-ventilated.

The soil is rich and alluvial; its level is below the sea, from which it is protected by embankments; it is transversed by majestic streams, on the borders and at the mouths of which dwell its inhabitants, and by numerous navigable canals. The climate is very humid; the temperature warm but equable; the prevalent winds are sea breezes from the east and north. There are two rainy seasons, the "little" from the latter end of November till January, and the "great" from the middle of April to the end of July; but during these periods there are breaks of fine weather, and during the dry season there are rainy days. A commentator says British Guiana is a tropical Holland.

The population of Georgetown (in 1837) was about 20,000. The prevalent diseases of the white population of Georgetown and British Guiana generally, are malarious afflictions of various kinds. Terrible epidemics of Yellow Fever have prevailed from time to time. Yet these attacks are separated by considerable intervals of time, which were filled up by the ordinary malarious fevers. In 1793 and again in 1819 severe epidemics of yellow fever occurred; but after the cessation of the latter in 1820, yellow fever seems to have disappeared so completely, that when the next epidemic occurred in 1837, the practitioners in Georgetown recognised the early cases simply from the description given of the disease in books. This entire disappearance of yellow fever in the intervals of the epidemics, from this low and marshy country, in which malarious diseases are never absent, is a point of great importance in the etiology of yellow fever. The last epidemic may be said to have lasted until the great rainy season of 1845, when it entirely ceased, being superceded by a slight but very general influenza.'

Christina's younger sister Marianne Shennan went out to Georgetown perhaps to be a companion when Christina was pregnant with her first child. Sadly though, Marianne died in Demerara, aged 31, on 19th November 1851 just a few days before the birth of the Knoxes' daughter.

By 1861, according to the Scottish census records, young Margaret Knox, aged about 9, was living in Edinburgh in her Uncle John Shennan's household with his young family at Bellevue Cottage, Broughton. She probably had been sent back to Scotland for her education and to be with her cousins of equivalent age. No other members of the William Knox family are to be found in the Edinburgh 1861 census.

A remarkable find in the Newspaper archives of the British Library is a despatch of some 2000 words from the *Inverness Courier*, 24th October 1864.

'A correspondent' gives this description of **Georgetown** …

'Georgetown contains, according to the last census … about 25,000 of a population. The town has an area out of all proportion, according to our European ideas, with the population. This arises from the fact that, save in one street, the houses are almost universally isolated, and have a patch of ground unoccupied, save by trees, between them and their neighbours. The houses are all built of wood, … The ground is too soft to admit of any heavy structure being erected upon it. …You must not think, however, because they are built of wood they are either shabby in their appearance or small in their dimensions, or brief in their duration. For the most part they are the reverse of all these. The house I am living in at present, which is no more than a fair specimen of the houses of the better class, has two storeys, besides the ground floor, which is occupied as a store or, as I am perpetually wounding their dignity here by calling it, a shop. The storey above has a drawing room, two bedrooms, a parlour, a kitchen, and a gallery upon it, each quite as large and roomy as the corresponding apartments of almost any house in Inverness. The first is indeed larger, because, from the nature of the climate, it is of great importance that the room where the family sit for the better part of the day should be large enough to occasion a considerable draught. One thing that strikes you greatly as you walk along the streets is the blunted appearance of the roofs of the houses, arising from the absence of chimneys. Of these there is only one for each house, and it is always at the back of the building, and not visible from the street at all. **My host tells me, that when one of his daughters – who is now in Edinburgh for her education, and who is a native of the colony**–went there first, she remarked that it was funny to see so many flowerpots on the tops of the houses!

By 1864, however, the whole family had returned to Edinburgh probably because Christina was ill. She died at 17 Leopold Place, Edinburgh on 9th May 1864, aged 48. On the death certificate the cause of death is given as 'of valves with distension of the heart and dropsy and asthma; two years paralysis of right side', suggesting she had been ill for some time.

As Christina's brother, John Shennan, is the Informant on her death certificate it is probable that William had already returned to Georgetown. Nevertheless, it seems the intention of the family had been to remain in Scotland as their furniture and William's books had been returned to Edinburgh.

William Knox had rented the separate upper flat of Bellevue Cottage for his family (and goods) by agreement with John Shennan. At some time also John had 'made large advances' of money to William – perhaps to tide things over until William could recover his funds from Demerara.

After Christina's death, William arranged with his brother-in-law that the three children should be looked after by their maiden Aunt, Margaret Shennan, and they remained in the flat at Bellevue Cottage. This arrangement had the added benefit that the children would be under the additional care of John Shennan and his wife, Jessie, who lived in the lower flat. The young Knox family would also have the companionship of their numerous cousins.

William thus returned to Demerara in 1864, probably because the person left in charge of William's business there, Dawes, was making a mess of it (as is hinted later in a letter of Alexander Shennan's to Georgetown). Another pressing reason may have been for William to recover his funds for repayment of the money lent to him in Edinburgh.

Another family tragedy happened in British Guiana. Christina's nephew, John Shennan, eldest son of John Shennan of Bellevue Cottage, had been recorded in the Edinburgh 1861 census as an apprentice joiner, no doubt in his father's firm. He went out to Georgetown, probably accompanying William on his return to British Guiana. However, John died there on 11th November 1864, aged 22. This must have been devastating for his father and family back in Edinburgh.

William Knox remarried in Demerara on 14th December 1865 at St Philip's Church Georgetown. His new bride was also called Christina – Christina Lucas Paterson, aged about 33.

A Paterson family website tells us about this Christina's background. She was one of the numerous children of JD Paterson, originally from Dumfries, by his second wife. Paterson was reputed to be one of three British Naval Officers who decided to remain in Guiana after the first British occupation of the territory in the early 1800s.

However, the second Mrs Knox had only a few months with her husband. William died on 26th July 1866. A Georgetown newspaper the *Colonist* reported:

'At his residence in America Street, this day, William Knox, native of Edinburgh, aged 56. Universally regretted. He was buried in Georgetown (at 6 o'clock in the morning).'

Christina the second then came to Scotland. For a while she was living with her stepchildren and Margaret Shennan in Bellevue Cottage. However, she later voluntarily moved out into furnished lodgings:

'to allow their Aunt Margaret to have sole uncontrolled custody of the orphans'.

The relationship between the three young Knox children and their stepmother seems to have been cordial. In May 1867, their Uncle Alexander Shennan wrote that:

'The 2nd Mrs Knox is living in lodgings in Albany Street, Edinburgh, from where her sister is to be married. Mrs Knox has requested that Maggie and Jeanie Knox and Mary Shennan (one of John Shennan's children) are to be bridesmaids – although of no relationship to the bride!'

Later, in January 1872, by which date Mrs Knox had moved to Dumfriesshire, Alexander wrote that:

'The three children with their Aunt Margaret had visited Mrs Knox in Dalbeattie and had enjoyed their visit greatly'.

Christina Lucas Paterson Knox died at Langlands, Dumfries on 17th July 1873, aged 41, and was buried at Tynron (Dumfries & Galloway Courier). In August 1873 Alexander wrote to a Mr Hunter in Georgetown:

'I doubt not you will have heard of an event of much importance as regards to Mr Knox's Trust Estate with the death of Mrs Knox at Dumfries on 17th July last. It would seem she had been ailing for some time with severe headaches and general lassitude and disinclination to exercise tho' eating well. ..... and her memory also seemed to be somewhat impaired – judging from the symptoms I should think that tho' her limbs were stronger, yet her Demerara illness had doubtless left permanent injurious effects on her brain and nervous system, predisposing her to cerebral afflictions.'

Alexander was relieved to observe from William Knox's Will that the second wife or her representatives had no further right or interest in his estate following her recent death.

The death of William Knox in July 1866 left his children orphaned, aged 15, 11 and 9. Although their father had, as described above, made provision with his brother-in-law for their guardianship following their mother's death, their financial future was now the responsibility of trustees. Two trusts were involved: their mother's Marriage Contract Trust and William Knox's Estate Trust.

By the terms of the marriage contract of Christina Graham Shennan, her elder brother, John, had been appointed as a trustee and, therefore, figured largely in the establishment of the Knox family back in Edinburgh before and after Christina Shennan's death. Matters became more complicated when John Shennan himself died unexpectedly in November 1866.

At this point the Reverend Alexander Shennan, as John's only brother and the remaining original Trustee, took over the main burden of his late sister's Marriage Contract Trust. By deed of assumption he added Mr Alex Hay, Christina's uncle on her mother's side, and a Dr James Douglas as co-trustees. However, the finances for the orphans were controlled by other trustees in Demerara, who administered William Knox's will and were legally in control of his estate in British Guiana and hence held the purse-strings of funds for the Knox children during their minority.

Copious correspondence exists from Alexander to the representatives of the 'West Indies Trustees' in the form of copies of the outgoing letters over the following 20 years. These were written at least quarterly, both to acknowledge receipt of funds sent regularly from Demerara and to send detailed accounts and vouchers for expenditure on behalf of the Knox children as administered by Alex Hay in Edinburgh. (He had a jewellery business with premises in Princes Street.) Any legal business required in Edinburgh on behalf of the young Knox children was carried out by another Uncle – James Nisbet, a solicitor (married to a sister of Christina Shennan's mother).

The exchange of correspondence between Edinburgh and Georgetown was between Alexander in his capacity as the principal trustee in Scotland for the children and a Mr Andrew Hunter in British Guiana. Hunter must have been a person of some standing in the colony as he had twice been Mayor of Georgetown.

In addition to business matters, these letters contain news of the progress of the children and their needs and welfare as they grew up. Also mention was made to wider matters of events in Europe and even the weather.

At the end of November 1870 Alexander wrote to Hunter referring to the Franco-Prussian War of that year:

'We have had cold, dull foggy weather lately. I was glad to hear that with you the weather was all that was desirable for the crops. I did not expect to find that in so short a time and at so great a distance you would be feeling the prevailing effects of the continental war so precipitately. The evil would be vastly increased if Russian complications also came up.'

Again, in March 1871, Alexander reported on the Knox children:

'When I last saw them they were looking well enough though rather feeling their arms painful and uneasy from the effect of the vaccination; this seems to be a very general precaution at present; though I don't find that there is as yet any increase of a marked character in the number of smallpox cases in Edinburgh. However there is no doubt it has become almost epidemic in several quarters both North and South. I suppose this may be regarded as one of the legacies left us from the months of war on the Continent, with its attendant famine, exposure, privation, ill-clothing, unwholesome food, etc.'

In November 1871, Alexander's report on the Knox children to Hunter includes the comment:

'When in Edinburgh very recently I saw the young folks. I believe they had all had colds ...It is really little wonder they had been "colded" for the weather lately has been so very changeable. For instance, yesterday we had some frost and today, wind, rain and mud providing a very disagreeable trio of disagreeables.'

The first problem to be discussed with the 'West Indies guardians' was the continued care of the orphaned children. Eventually it was agreed that they should continue to be looked after by their Aunt Margaret and remain in the Bellevue Cottage flat. Margaret Shennan kept a firm hand on the housekeeping costs. In April 1868 the Edinburgh trustees were able to report to Demerara that the entire annual outlay for the young Knox household had amounted to £240 8s 9d.

All was well with the accommodation until, in June 1872, the Knox children (and Shennans) had to move out of Bellevue Cottage: it was to be demolished to make way for redevelopment. After some discussion with the Demerara Trustees, it was agreed that Margaret Shennan and the Knox children would rent a new home at 7 Annandale Street, taken for two or three years.

The children were by now almost grown up; Maggie 20, Jeannie 17 and Willy 15. Alexander reported that they were settling in well, getting the furniture set up, carpets and floor cloths laid etc. and said of them:

'They are really lovable and affectionate children – one can hardly help thinking how fond and proud their father and mother would have been if they had been spared to see them as they are now.'

Later, in March 1873, Alexander commented to Hunter that:

'the enormous increase in price for the ordinary expenses of maintaining housekeeping, clothing, etc, etc, as might be expected' had resulted in increased costs of the Knox family household.

# Uncle George Knox

William Knox's younger brother George had also been established in British Guiana by the 1860s. Nothing has been found to indicate what business or line of trade he was in. He was married but without children and must have been quite comfortably off as he supplied funds for a piano for the young Knox children in Edinburgh. He also owned a property in Cassells Place, Edinburgh. George Knox was one of the co-trustees of William Knox's Estate Trust, in effect one of the 'West Indian guardians' for the Knox children. As such he was ready with his comments as to the housing and care of the children after the death of their father.

At the outset of Reverend Alexander Shennan's involvement with the welfare of the young Knox children, he wrote on 29th May 1867 to his co-trustee in Edinburgh, Alex Hay, commenting on a letter received from the Demerara trustees regarding the expense of keeping the household of the children and their Aunt Margaret: £400 to £500 per annum was cited. After much discussion in Edinburgh and across the ocean, it was decided that these high levels of expenses (incurred before Alexander's time as trustee) were caused by extra costs following William Knox's death including the repayment of loans to the estate of John Shennan. (As mentioned above the annual expenditure for the three Knox children was actually in the order of £250 per annum.)

In his first letter to Mr Hunter, dated 31st May 1867, Alexander adopted a rather frosty tone. It seems that George Knox had been commenting unfavourably in a letter about the Edinburgh trustees management of the young Knox children's affairs. Alexander quoted George's words:

'I do not wonder that my brother was always in arrears as you say – when the expenses were just double what he must have understood them to be, and my own experience of matters when at home, showed me how his money was squandered.'

Alexander continued to Mr Hunter:

'I felt quite uncertain whether to write directly to himself, or rather to you. I think it better to take the latter course as my observations if addressed to him might have a warmth and pungency of expression which I might afterwards regret.'

Alexander then quoted a comment made by his Edinburgh co-trustee, Alex Hay:

'his remarks are a slur against every member of your father's family'.

Alexander continued:

'I feel inclined to think that ... in penning (those lines) he was passing very serious reflections not only on our family but on his own deceased brother, on my sister Christina and on my noble and universally respected brother John.'

Things had calmed down a bit by the time of the next mail which brought a letter from Mr Hunter, that Alexander sent on to Alex Hay, with the comment:

'You will see he (Mr H.) makes no excuse for G. Knox's epistle further than one might say of some rude uncultivated boor. "Ah well, why pay any attention to such a person, he knows no better and there is a practical impossibility about getting a silk purse out of a sow's lug!"'

In a letter of September 1867 to Demerara, Alexander made reference to the fact that William Knox's valuable books were deteriorating because of not being stored properly at Bellevue Cottage for want of a decent bookcase. However, his main news was that the young Knox children were delighted as their Uncle George might be visiting them in Scotland in the near future. However, this proposed visit did not take place, for, at the end of

130

the year, news came from Demerara that George Knox's wife, Devonia, was 'so poorly' and that George himself was unwell. By a letter of 14th March 1868 news came that Mrs George Knox had died on 25th January at Georgetown.

In 1870 Alexander reported to Mr Hunter that:

'Uncle George has provided funds for a new piano for the young Knoxes, especially for Maggie.'

In April 1872 came the news that George Knox was to remarry, news which came unexpectedly upon them all and that he might indeed be visiting Scotland in the near future.

In November that year Alexander wrote to Mr Hunter that:

'the young folks were all on the *qui vive* anticipating the arrival of their Uncle George'.

Later that year Maggie, now 21, told her Uncle Shennan of her intention to be married to her cousin James Hume. Alexander grumbled to her that it all seemed to be widely known among the 'aunts', i.e., his Birkenhead and Liverpool sisters. Maggie had also written George Knox about her plans.

In a letter of 14th November 1972, Alexander commented to Mr Hunter, that Uncle George Knox might have misinterpreted the early marriage plans of his niece.

'your letter indicates certain misapprehensions as to the purpose of Maggie Knox's letter to her Uncle George. Mr Knox had quite overshot the mark in leaping to the conclusion that his niece's marriage must be in contemplation – I may safely say there is nothing of that kind in prospect at present. And you may depend upon it that when the Trustees know of anything of that nature being on hand, you will not be left without direct and speedy information of the fact.'

Alexander continued to explain that Maggie Knox, knowing that she had come into a legacy on becoming of legal age, 18, felt she was free to make her own decisions. This legacy of £100 had come from Mr Morison, her father's late partner in business.

Only two weeks later came the news of the sudden death on 9th December 1872 of George Knox on board the Royal Mail ship on passage to Britain, his boxes being retained at Southampton. He was 59. Alexander wrote to Mr Hunter in some anxiety for information as how George's recent second marriage and death might affect any legacy the Knox children might have expected from him:

> 'I suppose that ...you are now the one Trustee acting under William Knox's West Indian Testament. I do trust with all my heart that you may long be spared in connexion to the Trust as otherwise very serious complications and changes might arise. I have already had some experience of "Chancery" intervention and I hope I never have any more of it.'

Following the news of George Knox's death, Alexander visited a Mr Templeton at his office in Glasgow. Templeton had been one of the Demerara trustees for the Knox minors, but had recently returned to Scotland.

In November 1870, Alexander had commented somewhat sourly to Mr Hunter about Mr Templeton withdrawing from the guardianship of the young Knox children:

> 'I do think that, considering the place he held in Mr and Mrs Knox's friendship and the attentions they showed him – as I understand – he might have shown more interest in the affairs of their young orphaned family. I am not aware that he has once called to see them at the Cottage.'

However, the visit to Glasgow had been valuable. Alexander learnt from Templeton that, as regards the rights of widows, British Guiana operated under Dutch Law. Hence the widow gets half the deceased husband's estate in trust: the children the other. It was further confirmed by Templeton that the second Mrs George Knox was expressly excluded from trusteeship regarding the young Knox children under George Knox's will. Since British Guiana was under Dutch law as regards the rights of widows, he expected that the young Mrs George Knox would likely get one-half of George Knox's estate and he supposed that, in the same way, Mrs William Knox (the second) would have had half of Williams' property at least in life rent whether his Will had been made or not.

As Alexander wrote to Alex Hay:

'If this be a correct view of matters this would explain what has hitherto been rather difficult to understand; *viz* how William (*Knox*) should have left his (*second*) widow half his property in life rent and the same proportion for his young family.'

In 1873 Alexander and Alex Hay both sent encouragement to Hunter to appoint further Trustees in Demerara:

'to promote the security and best interests of the Minors'

In January 1874, Alexander received a copy of George Knox's will and professed himself to Mr Hunter as:

'annoyed and astonished: for the apparent interest he manifested in the young Knox minors, Maggie especially, I did think whatever provision might be made for the young wife that they would not be forgotten. That anticipation has been completely knocked on the head.'

# Mr Dawes

In Georgetown, Demerara, a Mr Dawes had taken over William Knox's business. He was originally in partnership with William and, probably, when the Knox family were initially in Scotland, he was left in charge.

George Knox must have taken more than a passing interest, for, in November 1870, Alexander commented to Hunter:

> 'I write in connexion with the Dawes arrangement with the West Indian Trustees which it seems Mr George Knox would now find fault with and wish to get rid of ...It is *post horam* as the lawyers say, to think for a moment now of disturbing an express legal arrangement made years ago with Mr Dawes, and which seems to have wrought well in the past and affords no more ground now ...for suspicion in regard to the future.'

In December 1872, Alexander reported to Alex Hay after his visit to see Mr Templeton in Glasgow:

> 'He states that up to the time of his (Mr T.) leaving the colony ... Mr Dawes has paid up the instalments due in the Stock in Trade and he does not appear to have any doubt that they will have been in course of payment since that time. Like ourselves he can see no weight or property in George's statements as to Dawes being favoured in not having been urged to keep up the regular instalments.
>
> Mr T. seems to think that, while <u>possibly</u> he may have had an occasional extension of the exact time for making payments, they will doubtless have been made. So far as he can understand from his correspondence and other information, he considers Dawes must be doing a fair stroke of business.'

In January 1873, after George Knox's death, Alexander wrote to Mr Hunter:

'Your remarks on the "McGill & Dawes" matter in connexion with Mr George Knox's likes and dislikes throws light on certain feelings and sayings of his which, as conveyed in kind of confidential way to Maggie, I could merely hint at and attach small importance to. I can quite understand that if he did not get things quite as he wished, he would not at all mince matters in indicating his dissatisfaction. However, he's gone and we shall not say further things in way of disparagement of him – possibly enough both in mind and body have long been feeling premonitions of that breaking up of the whole system which so unexpectedly issued in his decease on his way home.'

However, by the following year, it would appear that Dawes had failed in the business. In April 1874, Alexander commented to Mr Hunter:

'What of Mr Dawes? From your letter . . . it would appear he has been in difficulties or has stopped payments or something like that.'

This was followed in Alexander's letter to Mr Hunter in July 1874:

'They were rather startling advertisements which appeared in the Gazette you sent me intimating the complete collapse of Dawes as having succeeded to Mr Knox's business. I can hardly say the tidings were unexpected as different visitors from Georgetown had stated their suspicions of his solvency when they were visiting my sister and the young Knoxes.'

In March 1975 Alexander commented to Alex Hay:

'as to the unsatisfactory state of the Dawes matter I think there must have been a kind of infatuation on Mr Hunter's part in regard to the man, It will be an expensive infatuation for the Knox Estate.'

In June 1875 Alexander wrote to Mr Donald Currie (who had taken over administration of the trusteeship in Georgetown following the death of Mr Hunter):

'That business of Dawes is appearing to be a very unsatisfactory one. We sometimes have wondered that William Knox should have confided much in him, when he had not proved very trustworthy on the occasion of William and my sister coming to Scotland and had necessitated William's return to Demerara much sooner than he had anticipated – if indeed he then intended to return at all.'

# Maggie Knox

As mentioned earlier, Maggie had been sent home to Edinburgh to stay with her Uncle John Shennan and his family, no doubt for her education. She was recorded as a member of their large household at Bellevue Cottage in the 1861 census. She would have been nine or ten years old.

By the time of her mother's death and her father's return to Demerara in 1864, she was therefore about 14 and was being cared for, along with Jeanie and Willy, by her Aunt Margaret Shennan. It was decided to send her to board at Miss Stevenson's school in Edinburgh 'as she was getting rather beyond her aunt's control' – a typical teenager, even in those days?

In a letter of January 1868 to Hunter, Alexander commented:

'Maggie quite takes after her mother's appearance and even carriage ... When in Edinburgh I saw the three young Knoxes. They were evidently quite happy at home. Had they been my sister Margaret's own children, she could not have taken a deeper interest in their welfare or felt more attached to them ... Both Jeannie and Maggie bid fair to be capital musicians. How this would have pleased their Papa!'

By October 1868 Maggie, aged 17, had:

'a new position at the Institution as a teacher; she wishing to make some practical use of her own education.'

Alexander reported to the Demerara trustees:

'The Principal, Mr Oliphant, and the other authorities in the establishment have expressed their cordial approval of her conduct.'

At that time there were several educational establishments for young ladies in Edinburgh with 'Institution' in their title. According to the Edinburgh Post Office Street Directory for 1868, Mr Thomas Oliphant was headmaster of a school housed at No. 33 Charlotte Square. Close by, at No. 23 Charlotte Square was the 'Edinburgh Institution for the Education of Young Ladies'. At 8 Queen Street was 'The Edinburgh Institution for the Board and Education of Young Ladies' while 'The Institute for the Education of Young Ladies' was run by Miss Johnson at 9 Moray Place.

Alexander, the fond uncle, wrote to Mr Hunter in 1870:

> 'Maggie is really a winning, happy, accomplished girl. She is much of a favourite wherever she goes. Her Uncle George has caused her great gratification in respect of her new piano: a beautiful and powerful instrument ... Maggie has such a spirit that, although she has not been well, she overtakes her strength with her fun and daftness.'

With her siblings and like her Shennan cousins, Maggie spent some holidays, two to three weeks at a time, in Birkenhead with yet more cousins, the Humes, the large family of Alexander's sister Isabella; and, no doubt, the Humes visited Edinburgh. A consequence of this was the engagement or, at least, declaration of intention to get married, between Maggie Knox and her first cousin, James Hume. Alexander first wrote of this in November 1872 although the marriage did not take place until December 1875.

In May 1873, following the deaths of Alexander Shennan's children, Margaret and William, at Bathgate, Maggie Knox had been keeping house for Alexander while Jane Shennan was absent visiting old friends in Houghton.

In December 1874 Alexander wrote to Maggie's 'intended', James Hume:

> 'Maggie Knox made me aware of your formal engagement and also of the proposal that the marriage would take place in June. I do not need to tell you that I have no special liking for the Union of such near relatives, but as you and she have decided that matter for yourselves, I shall not stand in your way. Nothing remains but to give you my good wishes in the contemplated new relation betwixt you.'

Alexander then ticked James off for not having consulted Maggie's guardians in Edinburgh or Demerara. Alexander pointed out that this would not have happened if Maggie's father had been alive and that it was he, Alexander, and the other trustee guardians, who stood in his place.

Alexander continued with pertinent counsel. For instance, that one consequence of the marriage would be the breaking up of the Edinburgh household for the other two Knox children, as yet minors. Also advice was offered as to the funds that would be needed 'for, I do not say an elegant, but a comfortable home.' £260 to £280 per annum was what was advised.

In June 1875, Alexander warned Mr Currie in Demerara that Maggie's forthcoming marriage, date as yet not settled, would require the drawing up of a marriage contract for her, in addition to the looming winding up of the Knox minor trusts, so that he, Currie, should bear that in mind if contemplating any changes of investment.

Alexander was obviously very fond of Maggie as he signed off a letter to her in September 1875: 'But I must close with love and best wishes to Aunt Margaret, Jeanie and Willy. Of course, like a selfish thing you'll be intercepting lots of the same for yourself from aye your affectionate Uncle AS'

Maggie and James decided that the marriage would take place in December 1875. Alexander wrote James on 8th November 1875 warning him that time was short and that the West Indies trustees had a hand in the matter:

'The Trustees, holding the place of Maggie's Papa, will not give their consent to the marriage until all points in connection with her future rights under the Trust be fully set forth in legal form.'

On the 19th November 1875 Alexander wrote to Mr Nisbet (another uncle, a solicitor who was drawing up the marriage contract for Maggie). James Hume had rubbed Alexander up the wrong way, seeming to:

'be more mean and mercenary than he has shown himself hitherto.'

The following day Alexander wrote to his sister Jessie (Edgar) explaining the situation. James' widowed mother, Isabella Hume, had written Maggie from Birkenhead:

'Isabella has certainly set up her birse *(bristles)* at the Trustees in fine style for questioning James as to being trustworthy and honourable.'

Alexander went on to comment:

'No one has benefitted more from the legal provisions made on her behalf before marriage than Isabella herself. But for these all her property through our late father would have been lost to her and hers. All the Trustees are doing is to protect both sides financially should one predecease the other.'

On 6th December 1975, Alexander wrote again at length to his sister Jessie about the ins and outs of arranging the marriage contract for Maggie.

A week later, on December 15th, Alexander commented dryly to Mr Nisbet:

'I notice what you state as to Jas. Hume's "generosity"; certainly he has managed to do anything but elevate the general opinion of his character during his recent correspondence and the last effusion; gives no better notion of his business and common sense.'

The same day Alexander wrote to Mr Currie in Demerara:

'I shall not be entering at length into the matter (of the marriage contract negotiations) further than to say that while there has been some little difficulties on the point on James Hume's part ... the Trustees here have fully attended to Maggie's interests and have in a measure secured a *quid pro quo* in the event of her surviving him. These arrangements appear harsh and stringent in the way in which the legal mind endeavours to anticipate and make provision for possible eventualities and being Uncle to both contracting parties, I have felt myself in awkward circumstances.'

The wedding duly took place in Edinburgh on December 28th 1875 at 7 Annandale Street. Maggie and James were married by Alexander assisted by the Rev. Dr Morton, Maggie's minister at St James Place. (Report in the *Liverpool Mercury*, 30th December 1875.)

Alexander reported the event to Mr Currie a couple of days later:

'The whole affair was certainly very successful, everything going on nicely, myself and Dr Morton being the tie-ers of the indissoluble knot betwixt them and the result hitherto, that they are thoroughly happy with each other, each being, in the "tither half's eyes, a nonpareil." I should also say that after all the bickering and arguing over the precise conditions of the Contract, there has been no dryness or ill-feeling left behind – all seems most harmonious and pleasant.'

By April 1876, Maggie and James had settled into married life at 44 Forthill Road, Liverpool.

Alexander wrote to Maggie on 25th April 1876, after she had suffered some kind of minor accident. After discussing money business, he asked:

> 'How are you feeling now? I was glad to see from Jamie's letter that you were very much better again – only you may tell him from me that there was no use <u>deaving</u> a body (!) with that tremendous <u>hurray</u>!! with which he concluded his announcement of that gratifying fact. Does he imagine folks are deaf when he shouts in that quasi vociferous fashion! Ah, well, it's no wonder after all. When persons get long accustomed to have the usual <u>welcome</u> and <u>easy</u> <u>chair</u> and <u>pipe</u> all ready for them on their absence for a few hours from home, they find it a great change when any ailment or other hindrance breaks in on the happy and pleasant routine.'

By February 1877, Maggie and James had moved to 44 South Hill Road, Liverpool. Their first child, James Edgar Hume, was born there on 8th March 1877. Alexander wrote to Maggie on 29th May that year:

> 'And how is the <u>marvellous boy</u> coming on? I quite imagine you and Jim are perfectly convinced of the thing – as indeed beyond all question – that there never was <u>such a boy</u>. I hope he still continues strong, healthy and thriving.'

A year later, on 10th May 1878, Alexander ended a business letter to Maggie:

> 'By the bye, it's too bad of your son disowning you as his Ma, and only confessing to you being his Attie Decly. You should let him distinctly understand that such conduct so reprehensible and unnatural <u>can not be</u> <u>tolerated</u>.'

Their second child, Christina May Hume, was born on 25th May 1879. On receiving the news Alexander wrote to James:

'Your letter came duly to hand, intimating receipt of another <u>dovelet</u> to the dovecote. I hope mother and child continue to do well and will keep well and hearty. My word, your responsibilities are multiplying! And I hope with these the business will improve too. So to verify the saying that, where God sends mouths, He will also send the meat. I dare say you have no fear of that. So little Jamie was not so thoroughly well pleased when his nose was broken – well, that is by no means a pleasing operation for any of us. It is a long time since I remember a Mr Kirkwood declaring, – when a subject of a helper was first proposed to him – "No man likes to be superseded." Perhaps Master James will be disposed to rejoin – "Them is my sentiments to a T!".'

Later that year, in November, Alexander closed a business letter to Maggie:

'I was unaware until this afternoon that you had shifted your abode again. Surely Jamie and you are forgetting that three moves are as bad as a fire … How is the wee pet coming on and Edgar too – thriving I hope to the utmost wishes of their fond and enjoying payrients (*sic*).'

There is not much more in Alexander's correspondence about Maggie and James Hume. The rest comes from various other sources.

In the 1881 census return, the family was living at 27 Balls Road, Birkenhead. James was described as an iron and coal merchant, aged 33. Maggie (29) and two children were recorded, John Edgar, 4 and Christina, 1. Maggie's sister Jeannie Knox was also living with them. They had two maids.

Isabella Margaret Hume was born on 10th April 1881. Christina died on 27th April 1886, aged 6. William Walter Kenneth Hume was born on 23rd August 1888.

By 1891, the family were at Cable Road, Hoylake, Cheshire, James described as an iron merchant, with Maggie, James Edgar 14, Isabella Margaret 9, and William Walter Kenneth 2. The household also included Jane (Jeannie) Knox 35 as 'living on own means', a housemaid and a cook.

In 1901, Maggie and James were at 12 Oakdale Road, Waterloo, Great Cosby, Liverpool. James 53, was described as a Commission Agent. With them were Isabella Margaret 19, William WK 12, and Jeannie Knox 45, with one general domestic servant.

James Hume died at the age of 57 in October 1904. In the 1911 census, Maggie, 59, was living with her daughter, Isabella Margaret 29, clerk in the office of a Flour Miller, and son 22, now called Kenneth Hume, an insurance clerk. Jeannie Knox 50, was still with them. They were still in the Waterloo area, at 9 Neville Marsh.

William (WK) Hume died on active service on 31 July 1917: 'killed in action' in Belgium. He was a corporal with the 6th Battalion King's (Liverpool Regiment). James Edgar Hume died in 1935. He was married to Wilhelmina McKean ('Minnie Hume') but had no children.

Maggie Knox-Hume died at the ripe old age of 84 on 26th December 1934 in Crosby, Lancashire.

# Jeannie Knox

Jeannie suffered from deafness. This was likely to have been due to the history of *Retinitis pigmentosa* in the family, inherited through the female line. This hindered her education as it made formal schooling difficult.

The first mention of Jeannie Knox's deafness was in May 1867 when Alexander, writing to Georgetown, quoted from his sister Margaret:

'It would never do for Jeanie to go to a Boarding School (*as her sister was doing*). She is sometimes so deaf.'

Indeed there was talk of her seeing a doctor in Liverpool who had helped with the deafness of her cousin, William Hume. When she was 12, in October 1868, a tutor came to the house rather than her struggling to learn by attending Miss Stevenson's school.

In the autumn of 1870, the Knox family were visited by a friend from Demerara, a Mrs Cruger. This lady had asked Jeannie:

'If she would not go out with her to Demerara and thus try whether the voyage and a change to the tropics would benefit her hearing. A very definite shake of the head was the reply.'

In November 1871, Alexander wrote of Jeannie's deafness:

'making her especially in need of patience and affectionate good management on the part of those in charge of her.'

In a letter of January 1880, Alexander discussed the need to provide a new home for Margaret Shennan and the two younger Knox children following Maggie's marriage. He confided to Alex Hay:

'Indeed one special subject of anxiety with Jeanie ...was about giving up of the house (in Annandale Street). I need not say that in the past I do not regard [my sister] Margaret as being under any pecuniary obligation to the Knoxes. She has spent her energies in their behalf and devoted herself to their comfort and welfare in a way they can never repay and I dare say they are quite conscious of that and grant that, had she been their mother, she could not have been more attentive to their interests. Besides, her own money has gone into the house maintenance as well as theirs. But as you say, the time has come when she should have perfect rest *(she was 71)* and the care of others, beyond what Jeannie Knox, however willing, can either be expected or be able to do.'

In the event, by June 1880, Aunt Margaret Shennan and Jeannie Knox had gone to live in Birkenhead; Margaret with her sister Isabella Hume and Jeannie with her sister Maggie Knox-Hume. Meanwhile Willy went into lodgings in Edinburgh.

Jeannie Knox died aged 80, on 31st August 1935 in Crosby, Lancs.

# William Arthur Knox (Willy)

In January 1868 when Willy, the youngest of the Knox children, was 11, Alexander Shennan remarked to Mr Hunter:

'Willy is a sharp acting, handsome boy.'

Seven years later, in February 1875, Alexander wrote to his sister, Margaret Shennan, to say that it was about time that Willy be pointed towards entering some kind of business. While Alexander would have preferred:

'that he should have been a year or two longer at his education.'

He acknowledged that Willy's frequent absences from school through ill-health and other causes had left him much behind other boys of his age. As Willy did not appear to be inclined to knuckle down to his studies, the Knox trustees had agreed that he should at once be set to some trade.

Willy had expressed a preference for cabinet-making and upholstery. Although Finlay and Sons of Princes Street were part of the wider family circle (the Steeles), the trustees considered that the firm of Messrs JAY Scott held a higher position in the trade in Edinburgh than Finlay. Also Scott's terms for apprenticeship were considered to be more favourable; six years of training was required, rather than five, and at better terms.

A month later, Alexander wrote to Margaret to say that things were falling into place for Willy's apprenticeship. However, Alexander was irritated by the fact that Willy's cousin, James Hume, had been suggesting that he might find an opening for Willy in Liverpool or Birkenhead. Alexander and Alex Hay were of the same opinion on this – that this suggestion complicated matters and unsettled Willy's mind.

As Willy had already left the high school it was urgent that he be settled. Meantime it was suggested that:

'He should daily be doing some thorough work at his Arithmetic and useful reading and also improving his handwriting. Any little jobs about the house may also give him increasing facility in the use of tools.'

By May 1875, Willy was launched into his apprenticeship. Alexander asked his sister Margaret to get tougher on Willy:

'His pocket money allowance will now cease as he is making betwixt £7 and £8 yearly with his weekly wage'.

Also Uncle Alex was struck with the fact that Willy's clothing accounts have been more during the past year than Jamie and Hay Shennan's (*sons of John Shennan*) combined.

A year and a half later Willy again came into focus. Alexander wrote to Alex Hay about him on 20th November 1876; it appeared that Willy wished to attend evening classes in arithmetic, drawing and the violin. Alexander had told him that he must pay for these out of his weekly wages. Also the cost of:

'such things as wood for any articles of furniture he may make for sisters or others ... Willy seemed to think such things should be paid for out of the general household accounts ... How shall we manage in the case? He has so little idea of economising that if he had doubleheader would still use it all.'

Willy continued to exasperate his Uncle Alexander. On 20th November 1879, Alexander wrote to him:

'I have your note in course. You don't say whether you have received the note of the investments I sent you a few days ago – or whether you understand it fully, nor whether <u>you thank me</u> for <u>the trouble and time</u> <u>expended</u> in trying to put matters as clearly as possible before you and Jeanie. <u>Well, Well</u>!'

No doubt Alexander felt a particular responsibility for attempting to mould his nephew's future, as Alexander was Willy's only close senior male relative. Both the 'Birkenhead aunts' were widowed and, while the young Knox children had the benefit in growing up with many cousins in both Edinburgh and Birkenhead, the households in both places were headed by women.

A year later, in November 1880, Alexander replied to a communication from Willy:

> 'Your P. Card just received. How busy you must have been that, since I saw you last, you have had no time to write where you have been and what doing and what prospects.'

In December 1880 Willy, now aged 23, was lodging in London (11 Ravelston Road, Hornsey) with his cousin William Hume. It appeared that Willy Knox was looking for a position. Alexander advised:

> 'I need not urge you to be as economical as possible so as not to trench further into your capital …In going about any new situation you should not go as the young gent – having gold watch and chain: but rather in plain and simple attire as the young tradesman.'

Then in early 1881, Alexander found out that Willy had been discussing with Alexander's eldest son John Shennan about emigrating to America. *(See under John Shennan, Theodore's brother, for Alexander's reaction to this – squelching the idea as far as John was concerned.)*

However, it seems that Willy persisted in his scheme for going to America. In a letter of 15th March 1881, Alexander yet again tries to instil some gumption into him, while complaining that he, Alexander, does not know what is in Willy's mind as to an occupation. Alexander does not mince his words:

> 'No doubt you have now come to see the wisdom of the Trustees in wishing to have your education further advanced

before beginning business. The past cannot, however, be recalled and the best course for you is by hard study and self-education to make up your deficiencies in general information, reading, spelling, arithmetic and grammar. Of course, in educated and polished circles, the fact of writing an ill-spelt, ungrammatical letter would at once be set down as a black mark against a young man.

Now there is no lack of ability with you, but there is a lack of – what requires thought and self-application to hard toil. It may be a helpful spur to you to be told that Uncle Alec (Hay) was told by your superiors at Scott's (*where Willy had been apprenticed*) that you were very slow in your work and that you actually got worse in that respect in the last year you were in the workshops.

Now you may set yourself to the battle of life in earnest.'

Alexander ends this letter with an interesting comment about Willy:

'Your father set out for the far West with the two-fold aim to carry out with the paying off of his father's debts and with the support of Grandmother Knox. You know how ably he managed these two things, how much he was respected and how well he provided for his family.'

A fortnight later, Alexander writes again to Willy, who has had an idea about farming as an option:

'In your previous letter you spoke of going to America as a thing determined upon. As for trying the farming ...skill and attention and labour are just as much required in the far West as here. Now, you know nothing of farming and unless you intend for a season or two to be with a farmer, to see how things are managed, I doubt that hundreds and thousands may be swallowed up in the ground there. This has been the experience of an acquaintance of mine who went out to California or some other State there to farm and now I hear he is coming home again finding he had better just have kept his drapery business here.'

As Willy grew older he appeared to be in danger of coming under the influence of 'wild schemes', projects of doubtful calibre and which could hazard his inherited capital. He was also dismissive of his apprenticeship in cabinet-making calling it 'six abominable years at the bench' which prompted yet another exasperated letter from Uncle Alexander.

By April 1881 Willy, now aged 24, had abandoned thoughts of the going to the USA or Canada but instead had decided to go to Cyprus. There is no information of what project was involved, other than it was about farming and he required £200 (equivalent of £24,000 today) from his trust funds to finance this venture.

Willy's trip to Famagusta was to have been a two-year arrangement. It was to do with farming or land management in connection with a Mr Perkes. Alexander exhorts Willy in a letter of 12th January 1882 to do all he could as to learning about the crops and agriculture on the island. But by 25th January Willy is on his way home to Birkenhead. In a brief note to Willy at the end of March 1882 Alexander indicates that;

'the enclosed agreement with C. Perkes is hardly worth the paper it is written upon. Perhaps something might be made of the embezzlement of the money paid over.'

In May 1882, Willy had been offered an opening in Liverpool, to run a tobacco shop. There is no indication what exactly what this was to entail but, as Alexander writes to Willy:

'you have had no training for it and of course have no knowledge of the tobacco trade.'

In July 1882 Alexander indicated that, as regards the money for procuring a tobacco business, it seemed as though Willy wanted to tap into his sister Maggie's funds for the investment. However, by

September 1882, Alexander wrote to his fellow-trustee, Nisbet:

'You will see from the enclosed letter from WA Knox that he is now on a new tack and that the Tobacco business has lost its attractions now. The new area is in the Shipping Trade. He wants an immediate reply, but I think it better to have your view on the matter. In the event of his insisting on this new venture, could an arrangement be made for having the £600 in my hands of Maggie Knox-Hume's funds transferred to his in the security of one of his loans, at once, or as soon as he needs and the other £400 at 6 months, or so from the balance of such loans. I wonder what is to be the end of this drain on his resources.'

Alexander also consults Alex Hay on the matter and the result is all three Edinburgh Uncle Trustees blowing their top, led by a furious Uncle Nisbet. Alexander wrote on 8th September 1882 to Willy Knox:

'I have today received word from Mr Nisbet and he gives me his views (shared as he says by Mr A Hay) which are very much opposed to the "Shipping" adventure with Mr Robertson. For instance, he remarks, "I do not like his (Mr R's) proposal that W Knox should have the working of the accounts etc., while he looks after freights for him. What possible knowledge has W. Knox to work at Ships' accounts? None whatever. If the working of ship's accounts be such as easy matter, why should young men go to leave the trade of shipbroker or ship's husband. But with a ship everything beyond the mere navigating depends on the ship's husband and good trade and he knows nothing of that."

Then he proceeds "Surely he (Mr R) does not expect that £2000 i.e., £1000 for each, will suffice and if not we are not informed who are to be the other partners nor where the rest of the money is to some from. But has Mr R facilities to get freights in the Mediterranean trade?" Saying further that while "the shipping trade is still good

152

yet every one with powers of observation knows that with the number of ships building and built, a collapse is sure to come ere long and when it does come it will be serious for all concerned."

He adds, "W Knox is a trustee in his sisters Mrs Hume's marriage Contract. For the trustees to take over an investment held by one of themselves would in my view be injudicious at least." Then he meets the question, "What then are you to do?" Answers in "scotch fashion" by asking what did you leave the cabinet-making trade for? "Not to throw the trade at his feet after being through apprenticeship."

And his opinion is that throwing aside the appearance of being independent gentlemen, you should "put on workman's clothes and by hook or by crook, get into some thorough honest labour, perfect yourself in your trade, just till you can claim a foreman's place and after being some years in it look about you and gain experience of the world; then afterwards, but only afterwards, you may think of starting in trade for yourself and even then you may be better as servant (or manager) or such like as Master."

Such then generally are the views expressed by Mr Nisbet. And I quite imagine they may be unpalatable; at same time, "faithful are the words of a friend" and I cannot but feel they must be acknowledged as the shrewd, common-sense opinions of one who has your real good and success in life at heart. No doubt they suggest the work of ten or twelve years, possibly, of your future course. But even then you would, if then successful, be in a good or better position than your father was at the same age.

I suppose you could demand the paying up of monies invested on your behalf but the risk would be a most serious one until better grounds for the step be given than any you have yet had put before you. Do be patient. Don't expect all at once to step out of all present difficulties and discouragements and into a competency far less into an easily gained affluence. Trusting you will give due weight to these counsels and will be guided wisely aye your affectionate uncle, Alexander Shennan'

Willy's venture into shipping continued to occupy Alexander, who wrote to him on 7th October 1882 as follows:

'I have your letter of 4th current and now return proposed memorandum of agreement therein referred to with letter from Henry Robertson to (as I suppose) the present owners of SS Etna, agreeing to said Memorandum as her purchaser. You must take care that you do not find yourself in the lurches being a mere <u>lender of cash</u> to HR and not a <u>part owner</u> at all.

There is not any reference to you at all in the matter and the agreement, unless you have not copied it correctly, seems drawn in a loose and slovenly way – sometimes <u>buyer</u> is used and sometimes <u>buyers</u>, what is meant by what is contained in the 4th and 5th lines, on second page of Memo? It does not give sense at all on reading it – unless one puts "<u>before</u>" between the words "<u>sellers</u>" and "<u>transfers</u>" and <u>by</u> betwixt <u>insured</u> and <u>buyer</u>. Why not have filled in the true pressure on boilers? <u>I do think you should ask Mr Nisbet's</u> <u>advice as to its terms</u>. You have already lost enough without throwing another £600 away. Mr N is at home … I expect to meet him on Monday DV and will do what I can to expedite matters – but do gang warily.'

No further information has been found on Willy Knox's affairs. Alexander did not write again to him until July 1884. Willy was about to be married and Alexander sent his best wishes.

William Arthur Knox was married on 7th August 1884 to Janet Hay Easton. They had one child, Arthur William Easton Knox, born 29th November 1885.

Alexander Shennan's letters continue as far as the autumn of 1886 containing much detail on the management, particularly of Maggie Knox-Hume's funds. Sadly, however, with Alexander's illness, there the information ceases.

Willy Knox is mentioned in a letter of February 1897 from Theodore to his brother John in Great Falls Montana:

'I am glad you are going to keep Willie Knox where he is. He would just be a humbug if he came to Great Falls and live off you.'

In May the same year in another letter from Edinburgh to John, Theodore reported:

'An apparition in the shape of Willie Knox from Texas appeared Friday last. He is very thin, rather shabbily put on and fairly dome up but still the brisk look he had. He's come over about his aunt's money and is away down to stay at Waterloo (Liverpool) until September when he returns.'

William Arthur Knox died 23rd March 1910 in the parish of Hendon, Middlesex.

# The Trusts

Maggie's Funds of £1200 in 1886 are equivalent to about £157,000 today. This money was protected by her Marriage Contract Trust and came from her mother's Christina Graham Shennan's Marriage Contract Trust and from her father's funds held in trust by the Georgetown trustees. Therefore, it can be assumed that each of the three, Maggie, Jeanie and Willy Knox had equivalent capital from their parents. Hence the three Knox children were very well provided for.

CPSIA information can be obtained
at www.ICGtesting.com
Printed in the USA
LVHW040705040423
743358LV00001B/50

9 781789 633610